PRAISE

GRAPPLING

D1551421

"I *love* this book. The stories are page turners. I couldn't wait to see how each one turned out. And they are filled with learning. Bob has done a masterful job as a writer and a wise teacher. *Grappling* inspires and resonates profoundly."

—**Wendy Foster,** retired CEO, Big Brothers Big Sisters of Eastern Massachusetts

"Through the power of storytelling, Bob Kaplan shows us the myriad challenges that we all face in our personal and professional lives—and the effectiveness of true executive coaching that helps us get to know ourselves and improve!!!"

—**Jose Manuel Madero,** former CEO, Grupo Bepensa

"Drawing on his rich experience, Bob brings to life what it's like for executives to unlock their full potential. The stories, based on real people, are inspiring."

—**Jim Ryan,** retired CEO, Grainger

"Bob Kaplan has spent a lifetime helping executives improve themselves. In these interesting short stories, you will get a peek into how this complex process works."

—**Karen G. Ferraro,** Chief Human Resources Officer, Medline, 2012-2023

"Even if you aren't lucky enough to work with Bob directly, you'll benefit from these stories based on the struggles of real people just like you, who benefitted from the chance to dig deeper and make better choices about how to live their lives."

—**Bill Pasmore,** Professor of Practice, Department of Organization & Leadership, Teachers College, Columbia University SVP, Center for Creative Leadership

GRAPPLING

LEADERS STRIVING
TO IMPROVE

ROBERT E. KAPLAN

RIVER GROVE
BOOKS

Published by River Grove Books
Austin, TX
www.rivergrovebooks.com

Distributed by River Grove Books

Design and composition by Greenleaf Book Group and Teresa Muñiz
Cover design by Greenleaf Book Group and Teresa Muñiz
Author photograph by Karl Steiner

Publisher's Cataloging-in-Publication data is available.

Print ISBN: 978-1-63299-886-6

eBook ISBN: 978-1-63299-887-3

First Edition

CONTENTS

FOREWORD

Grappling: Leaders Striving to Improve is an important and unique contribution to the field of leadership development, replete with valuable and actionable insights for anyone who is a leader or wants to become one.

Bob Kaplan brings thirty-five years of experience in leadership development to writing this book. But we, as readers, never receive his golden rules on how to be a leader, or even how to improve as leaders, until the final chapter.

Instead, we are immersed into eight different situations, all of them fraught, that take place over an extended period of time. In each story, valued corporate executives are experiencing problems in their leadership, and their CEO, board member, or head of human resources has engaged an outside expert to help the individual identify their roadblocks and find a pathway through.

Using fictionalized stories based on real-life clients, the author illuminates the myriad ways high-performing executives can undermine themselves with counterproductive behaviors and beliefs that they may not recognize, or even deeply believe are important to their success.

We meet a CEO fixated on an unworkable strategy, an executive who can't handle pushback, and a brilliant technology leader who can't stop spewing knowledge. At the other extreme, we encounter a CEO who has trouble leaning in, a division head who lacks confidence in their interpersonal relationships, and a turnaround executive focused on results but not people.

Another powerful insight from the author, highlighted in this book, and central to the author's methodology in leadership development, is that we are the same person at home and at work, because our beliefs and habits have deep, emotional roots.

Does the hard-driving executive, who uses criticism and fear as motivators at work, and who comes home to the news that their eight-year-old got a failing grade on a test at school, say to the child, "Hey, what do you think happened, sweetie? Do you want to talk about this? Not now? Well, come give me a hug. Of course, I am not mad at you. I just want to help where I can." Probably not.

With everyone's permission, the executive coaches in each story explore both the corporate and family dynamics using a 360-process that includes interviews with the struggling leaders, their coworkers (bosses, peers, direct reports), and their family members (especially the spouse, as appropriate).

We witness some dramatic epiphanies as the leaders receive positive and negative feedback, recognize unhelpful tendencies at work, and also realize how they create difficulties at home. At the same time, Bob illustrates how the family's involvement can bring important support for changing and provide additional opportunities to practice more effective behaviors and develop new habits.

As you read the stories, you will find Bob calling himself and his colleagues "guides," instead of coaches. I can see why he might do this—doesn't our image of a coach come mainly from sports, where they yell at the players from the sidelines, even calling their next plays? At a deeper level, this approach is supported by decades of experience in multiple areas of learning. As Bob tells us, and illustrates in the stories, struggling leaders can have greater and more durable success, not by being told, but by using their own answers to an expert guide's well-timed and well-framed questions to identify the problem areas, and the possible solutions, themselves.

One of the best aspects of this book is that Bob also applies this approach to us, the readers. He plunges us straight into each story, without offering side comments or interpretations that might put us in a better position to understand. Instead, we learn things at the same time as the people involved, so we directly experience the struggles of the leader and family members as they (and we) try to grapple with the problems and grope for resolutions. We witness the challenges of changing and celebrate any breakthroughs with them—when they happen, if they happen. Because in life, and in this book, meaningful and necessary change is difficult, and not everyone gets there, or all the way there.

Bob also shows us how executive coaching works—that guides are also human beings, with needs and habits that they have to control, just like the executives they are trying to help. We see his guides deciding how to interact with the executive and the family, constantly trying to find the right question, the right connection, to help the leader understand.

In the final chapter, though, while the author still does not analyze the eight stories for the specific lessons we should be drawing from each one of them, he does give us an excellent road map for how we can assess and adjust our own performance, at work and at home, in the spirit of continual improvement. The tone is light, but, as he tells us, the work is hard.

The headlines in this final chapter underscore the process and approach we experience in his stories, including "Find Out What You're Up Against," "Factor in Childhood Influences," "Be Open to A Character Shift," "Heed the Positive Feedback," and "Involve Your Partner."

His pivotal point for me is that we have a mindset that affects our choices, and his analogy is wonderful: If "drive for results" is as big as Brazil on your mental map, he tells us, while "patience with people when they occasionally screw up" is smaller than Lichtenstein, then we will be doing a lot of the former, and not much of the latter. (A helpful framing for everyone except the geographically challenged.) And, he says, because change is uncomfortable, it may take a guide to help you. I wholeheartedly agree and recount a personal experience at the end.

Nothing in this book is unintentional, from the name, *Grappling: Leaders Striving* to Improve, to the design of the front and back covers.

When we grapple, *Merriam-Webster* tells us, we can be using an instrument to grab at or grip something, and the main title word, *Grappling*, runs straight up the left side of the front cover, like a rock face we are climbing. *Merriam-Webster* also tells us that, when we grapple, we begin to understand or come to grips with something in a direct and effective way—like the leaders, and sometimes the spouses, in this book.

We also learn in the preface that the book subtitle, *Leaders Striving to Improve*, is the modus operandi of our author, who admits to being highly competitive and constantly working at getting better. Then, he gives us the evidence right on the back cover, by using a recent, candid, photo of him running as hard as he can on the beach. Why? Because, as he tells us, he is constantly striving to improve, in everything.

I am a scientist, entrepreneur, and executive with forty years in the biotechnology and medical device industries. And, like Bob, I am physically active—hiking, skiing, traveling, urban walking, and weight-lifting. I live in a four-story house in San Francisco, and I have taken to running up the stairs to save time.

I began my career in scientific roles, then also took on various business roles. This broader experience helped me cofound the medical device company, Kyphon, in 1996. I served in numerous capacities, including start-up CEO, Chief Science Officer, and board member, and remained to help with the transition after its sale to Medtronic in 2007. I retired from Medtronic at the end of 2010 because I was elected to be an executive board member for the healthcare nonprofit, the American Diabetes Association, ultimately serving two separate years as board chair. I currently serve on the board of Glyscend (a clinical-stage biotechnology company where I met the author), advise two early-stage healthcare-related companies, help young healthcare entrepreneurs, and continue my involvement with healthcare non-profits.

I have learned from my own experience the value of working on yourself with expert help. While the author was conducting the behavioral research in the 1980s that led him to incorporate the client's broader life into his leadership development approach, I was a young scientific leader in the early days of biotechnology.

Our new CEO recognized that the senior team had talented people but with limited corporate experience and engaged respected organizational experts/coaches to help all of us develop a greater understanding of ourselves and of good management practices. We brought our real-life work problems to the group sessions and role-played how to address them. I realized how these approaches could help me in my family life as well.

One of my obstacles at that time was a senior colleague who would strongly (and I felt unreasonably) challenge my results or interpretations during monthly scientific reviews. I would feel ambushed and react defensively. Worse yet, our colleagues saw the tense interactions and thought the problem came from both of us. Through leadership coaching, I recognized that I could not change that colleague's behavior, but I could change my own. The next time it happened, I reacted differently. Even though I still felt ambushed, I was able to answer calmly, simply pointing out the various aspects of my presentation that had already directly addressed the question. At the end, as we all left the room, I was happy, and relieved, to overhear one colleague quietly say to another, in essence, "Did you hear that gotcha question? It was unnecessary and a little rude, but Karen handled it well." This skill continues to serve me.

Most assuredly, if you are leader with challenges at work and are given the opportunity to work with an executive coach, you are very fortunate. At the same time, whether you have a guide or not, this book can help you understand common roadblocks and more effective leadership practices, as dramatized in the eight distinct stories, and enhanced by the road map and general guidance that the author provides at the end.

Happy Reading, and Happy Grappling!

Karen Talmadge, PhD
Cofounder, Kyphon, Inc. (bought by Medtronic)
2013 Chair and 2018 Chair, Board of Directors,
American Diabetes Association

PREFACE

Have you done much grappling with yourself? I have done my fair share of it. As father to my three precious children, now adults, I struggled with impatience. I've had to guard against working too much, especially with kids at home. I'm intense and at risk of getting carried away on any playing field. I watch myself, guide myself, and I'm always striving to improve at whatever is important to me. I have also done my fair share of helping other people grapple with themselves. These have mainly been leaders but sometimes a family member or friend if they wanted my help.

My one-on-one work with leaders goes all the way back to the late 1980s, when my colleagues and I at the Center for Creative Leadership came up with a prototype of executive coaching well before there was such a thing. The service was a by-product of an R&D project on the development needs of senior managers. We used a novel methodology, what we called *biographical action-research*. We used *action-research* in the sense that you study a phenomenon by changing it or attempting to change it. *Biographical* was in the sense that we took into account the leader's early life and current life. Since then, whole-life consulting to senior managers is largely what I've done—in large organizations and in start-ups (www.kaplandevries.com).

I have also done plenty of expounding on the topic: many articles, several books—a lot of exposition in the form of theory, research findings, advice, and case studies designed to make a conceptual point. Lately, I found myself yearning for another way to convey what I've learned, and I hit on the idea of writing novelistically. The narratives that follow are based on real people, and, as with historical fiction, many of the scenes are imagined. The narratives are instructive, but the instruction is implicit; it's not spelled out. The closing chapter, "Lessons for Leaders," however, makes explicit the themes that cut across the several narratives.

You will encounter a variety of leader types, even archetypes. You won't just witness these leaders in the office. You will get to follow them into their homes. You will see that, whatever the arena, their basic character is always in play, for good or ill. Their character is also revealed in the way they relate to the trained professional—the guide—attempting to help them grapple with themselves.

Each of these dramas is unique, but they have in common the universal struggle to do better and be better—to mature. Maturity is not just knowing your worst tendencies but getting a handle on them.

Sam, a turnaround artist, has the mentality to match, which is deeply ingrained, and plays out everywhere.

WRONGED

S am Calastri sat high in his black leather desk chair behind his massive white oak desk, completely free of paper and polished to a gleam that almost hurt your eyes. A big man, looking fit and strong though no longer young. He came to work every day in a dark suit and white shirt, senior management's uniform, but his tie was always loosened.

Opposite him stood two straight-backed chairs for guests. In one perched Sally Cain, a self-described guide to leaders, who had flown in from Boston. To her own black corporate outfit Sally added a splash of color, a classy scarf loosely knotted and draped over her shoulders.

Sam had cancelled twice before. The first cancellation she accepted without question. The second one made her doubt his commitment. That, or he was just jerking her around.

The top HR executive, along with the CEO, had decided to get consulting help for an *enfant terrible* in senior ranks, not Sam. To avoid the appearance of singling out the problem executive, they decided that a senior person in good standing should "work on themselves" at the same time.

The CEO himself was the best choice, but he demurred. So the HR head approached Sam—the two of them went way back—and Sam agreed. It fit. Sam had always beaten his brains out to make the grade, and that always meant learning new things, acquiring skills. Hence Sally's presence in Sam's office, although she knew none of this backstory.

As Sally attempted pleasantries, Sam had his chair tilted back. He wasn't going to make it too easy for her, or it wouldn't be a true test. Coddling people, like his children—he had three—was antithetical to him, abhorrent. He had no truck with presents for children whose birthday it wasn't.

For Sally, it was like scouting around for a foothold on a sheer rock face. *Surely, there's a dimple, the slightest indent, something to support my weight.* Her breathing was shallow; her diaphragm hardly moved. She thought to ask, "How did you come by this big job?"

Now his chair came vaulting forward, his deep voice filling the room. She'd hit on the thing that animated his very being. "Long story short: I had my heart set on a company with a dominant market position—Stellar Corp, a medical device business, in particular. Coming from some no-name rinky-dink college, I had no business applying there. For some unknown reason, they hired me."

She wanted to say, *Good for you,* but doubted it would be welcomed. She wasn't a rookie. After getting a master's degree in counseling and going to work at a search firm with a newly added consulting arm, she'd put in the 10,000 hours that's said to be required to get good at something—not to say she'd completely mastered her discipline or herself. When she was just a baby, her paternal grandfather heard her piercing cry and predicted she'd be an opera singer. Her maternal grandfather referred to her at age three as "a tornado." Her father, stunned that at a young age she escalated when they admonished her, said she "raises Cain."

"Foot in the door at Stellar, great," Sam continued. "But then it was up or out. I had zip chance of making the first cut. At least that's what the other guys in my entering class of twenty-five management trainees seemed to think. They never missed a chance to drop the name of the fancy school they'd gone to. They looked at me like I was some ugly duckling. Maybe it was my crewcut. No one else had one."

She felt for him but kept her mouth shut. *Let the line run out*, she told herself. She'd gone deep-sea fishing a few times past Georges Bank.

"But, truth be told, they were much better prepared than me— bigger vocabularies, more articulate. I had so much ground to make up it wasn't funny. Worked ninety hours a week. Kept it up 'til Christmas, and then I was sick as a dog—high fever, raging sore throat. Then back at it 'til the Fourth of July and sick again. I should never have taken time off.

"A year into it, my peers were getting promoted, and I wasn't. Scared the daylights out of me. But my supervisor taught me the ropes. If it weren't for him, I'd never have made the cut." He got choked up for a moment.

Sam scooched back a little and opened the drawer. Out came a switchblade. With the tip of the blade, he scraped dirt from under his fingernails. *Like killing a flea with a cannon*, she thought. Growing up, she'd owned a jackknife, skinned branches, played mumblety-peg with the neighborhood boys. She wanted to tell him that, get her lips unstuck, but she refrained.

"It's grease," he explained. "I do all the work myself. It's an old pickup truck, a Ford F-150. A wreck when I got it. Rebuilt it myself, body work and all. I promise you it's the only truck in the parking garage."

Common-man touch, she thought. "I'd love to see it." Finally, she got a toehold in the conversation.

"You can do more than that; you can drive it. If you can handle a stick shift, that is. This one's on the floor."

"No problem. That's how I learned to drive; that's how my kids learned." *Take that*, she thought. Emboldened, she tried a segue. "Do you work on yourself?"

"You bet. Every new job I get, I whip myself into shape. Have to." At *whipped*, Sally raised her eyebrows. Evidently, he read that as wanting to know more and added, "I bone up on the new business, do a SWAT analysis on it."

Hesitantly, she asked, "How about, you know, self-improvement?"

He blinked. "You mean style issues? But why would I mess with a winning formula?" She sensed he was toying with her. "Like I told you on the phone, I don't introspect much. That's why you're here."

"Yes, that is why I'm here," she said, grateful to have her reason for existing confirmed yet fearful he was just putting her on. The photograph on the wall behind him caught her eye—a young man in a football uniform. "Is that you?" she asked, pointing. *Stupid question: Who else could it be?* But again, she had hit on something core to his being, and he didn't bother to tease her.

"Yeah, I played for a very good Michigan State team that won the Big Ten title my senior year." He smiled, revealing a crooked tooth next to his front tooth. *No money for orthodontia.*

"My college boyfriend played pro football."

He perked up. "Which position?"

Ah, good. I've got him, she thought. "Defensive back. For the Bengals."

Not to be outdone, he said, "I played middle linebacker. Pity the ball carrier I got my hands on." His eyes flashed like he was getting ready for the ball to be snapped.

"Well," she said, "I played varsity hockey in high school—defense." She got to her feet. "I'm not that big—as you can see—but I spent plenty of time in the penalty box. Mighty Mouse, my teammates dubbed me." She could be faulted for getting down to his level, or you could applaud her for helping herself with him by drawing on what she had in common.

"Scrappy, huh?"

"Yes, that was said." *What—am I winning him over?* She sat back down and began to breathe a bit easier. But not content with the win, she kept pushing, uneasy as she did it. Her husband told her she didn't know when to quit. "Your style of play as an athlete," she said, "how does that compare with your leadership style?"

"You're right, Sally, I wear the black hat."

"The black hat—what does that look like?"

"It looks like my Darth Vader costume." She couldn't tell if he was being literal, but he was. Literally, every Halloween he wore it—never tired of shocking people new to the Halloween parties he and his wife threw, rollicking affairs. "Want to see the black hat in real time? Sit in on my ten a.m. meeting tomorrow. You're invited." She accepted, thinking it would help to see him in action.

The following day, after waking up, she stayed in bed, eyes closed.

Her father came to mind. He smoked, and when she was seven, she told him, with the moral clarity of a child that age, "Dad, smoking's not good for you. You've got to stop." He kissed her on the forehead and did stop. A few years later, his drinking caught her attention. That he drank—martinis, wine at dinner—wasn't new. It was that he probably drank to excess. Again, she appealed to him. Again, he thanked her, hugged her affectionately, but this time nothing changed. Frustrated, she kept after him, but that only served to displease him, and she didn't want that. Getting dressed, she mused, *Why did I think of Dad? Does Sam remind me of my father?*

The occasion for the ten o'clock meeting: Stellar had just issued a recall on a new type of replacement hip. When he got word of the recall, Sam was mortified; he was furious.

Someone had brought over a couple of extra guest chairs, and Sally took a seat in one of them. "Don't mind her," he began, shooting Sally a bad-boy grin, "she's a shrink." She welcomed being recognized but not in that way. Normally, she'd object to *shrink*, but she was mollified by his humor.

The GM, a fellow named Charlie, started passing around a slide deck, but Sam interrupted him. "What's the point?" he barked. "You sent this out as a preread. Everyone read it, right?" Whether they had or hadn't, people nodded sheepishly. "So what have you found? What do you recommend?" Charlie turned to one of the staffers, a young woman so nervous her hands shook. Sam heard her out and, softening his tone just a bit, said, "Thank you, Lisa," then turned to the R&D head. "This analysis is full of holes that even a nontechnical guy like me can see. It's not ready for showtime, and you know it. Get back to me tomorrow," he boomed. It was Thursday.

"But, Sam," the R&D lead protested weakly, "that's not enough time."

"Okay. Monday." With a wave of his arm, he dismissed them.

Just then, Sam's phone rang, and Sally, having had an eyeful of black hat, saw her chance. She waved good-bye and ran after the GM, Charlie. "Can I ask you something?" she said, out of breath. "Is he always this way?" He nodded and ushered her into his office.

"That's him. He gets angry, but it blows over quickly. It's his 'this isn't good enough' approach. We're used to it, most of us anyway. If you can't take it, you leave. Plenty of people have left. By the way, I'm one of the chosen ones. Every time he's given a new assignment, he's taken me with him."

"What's the attraction?"

"Despite the hard exterior, he's got a good heart, which he does his best to hide. It pains him to let people go, especially first-line employees. But he gets called in to fix businesses, and that means triage. It's brutal, but it's his job to be brutal."

Sally and Sam met for dinner at Morton's, his favorite steak place. "Listen," he said, "I'm not the complete asshole you must think I am." That devilish grin again. "Not that I give a damn."

She turned mischievous herself and asked, "Do you have proof?"

He stared at her for a moment. "Okay. Our youngest, Brian, who's fourteen—last night, he and I watched the first half of Thursday Night Football together. It was the Steelers, our home team, against the Patriots."

Taking after his father, Brian played football. Sam's wife, Margaret, had objected. "Football ought to be outlawed," she had said.

"First let's outlaw war," Sam fired back.

During a commercial break, Brian had muted the TV and said, "Dad, call my cell phone."

"'What the heck for?' I asked. 'I'm sitting right here.'

"'Just do it, okay?'"

"He handed me his phone, and it rang with an ominous, dun-duh-duh-dun. Beethoven's Fifth, I think. His way of ribbing me about my—what's the word?—persona. I leaned over and punched him on the shoulder, lightly of course."

"That's your idea of camaraderie?" She teased him, although she sensed faintly he was touched by the moment but wanted to hide it.

"Hey, the kid knows. Who says it has to be hugs and kisses?" It sounded like he was offended, but the glint in his eye said otherwise. Banter was his favorite indoor sport.

"Are you that way with your wife and daughters too?" Even though she was still unsure of her position with him, she too enjoyed the repartee.

"What do you take me for?" he said and slid his phone over to her. She caught it as it was about to fall off the table. "Here. Talk to my wife. Ask her."

Shaking her head, she slid the phone right back, noting with pleasure it stopped just short of the edge. *What—are we playing hockey?* "In due time," she said, worried he'd persist.

"Okay then, I'll tell you what she'd say."

Before he could put words in his wife's mouth, Sally interjected. "Are you open to a counteroffer?"

He raised his chin, signaling her to go ahead.

"I have a better idea. Let her tell me directly."

"Fine by me." She was taken aback, not prepared for him to

agree and so readily. *What's going on? Am I turning the corner?* She smiled inside, and the glow showed.

"Just so you know," Sam threw in, "Margaret's a handful. She catches fire way too easily."

Look who's talking, Sally thought, but much more charitably than she'd have felt a minute earlier.

In short order, Sally arranged to meet with Margaret, in a conference room at her hotel. Margaret interrupted before Sally could get two words out of her mouth: "I get it. I'm a psychiatric social worker—at a prison, actually." Murderers, rapists, the muscle-bound types—she could handle it, although, sometimes too quick with a comeback, she got herself in hot water. "What's Sam like? To the kids, he's Father with a capital F. He plays hardball with them."

"What would Sam say?"

"'When it's needed.' I don't always see the need. Case in point." She related a recent incident involving their fifteen-year-old daughter, Lisa, their middle child, a high school sophomore, a natural high achiever. In Margaret's telling, Lisa had burst into the kitchen, knocking the swinging door into the wall. Margaret jabbed her index finger at the phone in her hand. Lisa paced the floor. The moment Margaret put the phone back on the hook, Lisa rushed up to her (Sam preferred wired lines, better sound quality). "Mom," she shouted, "Dad is on my case about my fall-term grades!"

"What did he actually say?"

"That there was no excuse for a B. That I ought to try harder!"

Margaret tried to calm her down. "Can I get you something to drink?"

"Diet Coke."

"It's too late for caffeine." Lisa settled for a caffeine-free Dr Pepper.

They sat down at the kitchen table; Margaret squeezed her daughter's hand. "Look. You may find this hard to believe, but your father is very proud of you."

"You'd never know it!" Lisa said and stomped out of the room.

Sally was about to ask how the two of them met, but Margaret beat her to it. They met in college, and at first, Margaret was in awe of him. He was a senior, she just a sophomore. He was the starting linebacker on State's winning football team. She couldn't hold a candle to that. But once they were married, right after graduation, and once she got an eyeful of his feet of clay, the awe wore off quite a bit, and gradually, she learned to stand up to him.

From the beginning, one of Sam's favorite ways to show he cared for Margaret was to surprise her. For their twenty-fifth wedding anniversary, they'd treated themselves to a long weekend in New York City. He'd led her to believe they would stay at their usual perfectly fine hotel, the Kitano. But, after dinner, he suggested they pop over to the Four Seasons for a nightcap. Walking in, they both admired the temple-like lobby. Then Sam took her by the hand and headed over to the registration desk.

She grabbed his arm. "What's going on, Sam?!" He allowed himself to be stopped, turned slowly around, and flashed a big smile. Catching on, she rushed into his arms.

That concluded Margaret's account. She turned to Sally. "Give you an idea?"

The whole time Margaret was speaking, Sally had been scribbling away. "It does. Thanks," she said. "I'm guessing you told Sam about how upset Lisa was?"

"You guess right. I pointed out the error of his ways. He didn't want to hear it. I could help him grow, but he's not open to it. It's a shame."

Sally cleaned up her notes and showed the transcript to Margaret, who was amazed Sally had got it down word for word. She gave Sally permission to show it to Sam.

At her next opportunity Sally, feeling like she was firmly in charge of the situation, did just that.

Sam read the transcript and said, "Yeah, that squares with what she told me about it. My older daughter could take it, and she performed at the highest level. McKinsey made her an offer, and they only hire the best and the brightest; she preferred to go in-house. You've got to challenge your kids. Parents these days are way too protective. Margaret's not the worst, I have to admit."

"What about the last part—when she caught up with you?" Sally asked, thinking *Sam's letting me do my job, and that's all I want.*

He threw up his hands. "Typical Margaret. Here's what actually happened. She walked into my home office one evening, and she was so upset I could hardly make out her words. I got her to calm down enough to tell me what happened. That part I bought."

"Do you buy that she could help you grow?"

He snorted. "Yeah, she tries to play therapist with me. Spouse as therapist—not a good idea. Anyway, she's clumsy. Gives me gratuitous advice; nobody wants that. And she tells me what I'm feeling. How would she know? I know she's better than that at work."

Margaret's clumsiness excited a touch of schadenfreude in Sally. But mostly, she was excited about the headway she was making with him and more intent on helping him. In all the sparring, she hadn't lost focus on that. In fact, she was getting clearer in her mind on how best to be useful.

"Sam, Margaret suggested I ask you about your father. Urged me to do that."

He sighed. "Do you want that?"

"Yes, very much: The child is father to the man, you know. But I'm mainly interested in you, the effect on you."

"He was hard on me and on my mother too—when he drank. A six-pack—Pabst Blue Ribbon, the local beer; we lived in Milwaukee. Slugged them down one after the other. Then, watch out. He could turn ugly in a heartbeat."

"Can you be specific, if you don't mind?" She trod lightly. No telling what was next. No telling how bad it was.

"He didn't hit me, if that's what you're wondering. Once or twice, he rapped my knuckles when I was late for dinner, but that doesn't count. There was one time when I disobeyed my mother when she told me to babysit for the younger kids. I shook my head no and darted off to play ball with friends anyway. 'Disobey your mother again,' he told me later, towering over me and hopping mad, 'and I'll kick your ass.' But he never did. That reminds me: My brother calls me the 'Cosmic Ass-Kicker.'" Sam smothered a smile.

"Your dad turned ugly but no problem?"

"I got used to it. What do you want me to say?" She looked doubtful. "Know the song, 'A Boy Named Sue'?"

"No, but I get the idea."

"Yeah, my father toughened me up. He's a big reason I've done as well as I have."

She emitted a little wordless *hmmph*.

He took offense. "What—you don't believe me?!"

"It's not that." She paused for a moment. "Only upside?"

He thought about it. "You mean I'm putting lipstick on the pig?"

"Pretty much," she said, brightening. *Getting somewhere!*

His daughter Kathleen, twenty-four, reached him that evening and the same themes got struck. In her midtwenties, Kathleen had followed her father into the business world. "I've been promoted to team leader, and I don't know a thing about managing people," she told her father.

Neglecting to congratulate her, he said, "You'll do just fine. You're organized. You have a good touch with people. Get some experience under your belt, and then we'll talk."

"I want to model myself after you."

"Oh, I wouldn't do that. Do as I say maybe, not as I do."

"Nothing wrong with the way you lead, Dad."

"What do you know about the way I lead?" He brought the hard edge, but she had long ago adapted to it.

"I've heard the stories. You attack what's wrong; it energizes you, right?"

"I can't deny it. But you, you're a much nicer person than I am."

"At work, don't be so sure. The apple doesn't fall far from the tree."

Oh great, he said to himself, but he was pleased too.

The Alcohol Factor

Sally had a very particular reason for dropping by Sam's office the next day. "There's something I want you to know. My father drank too." *How about that!* he said to himself. "But I don't mean to equate our situations; my father's personality didn't change when he drank. Either way, he was a pretty darned good father."

It was Sam's turn to be doubtful. "Let's say it was benign, his drinking. Even so, did it have an effect on you?"

She got her back up. "What am I supposed to compare it to, a hypothetical father I didn't have?"

"Never mind." He was tolerant. Having drinking fathers in common helped with that. But with a twinkle in his eye, he then said, "Types like you aren't supposed to be defensive, are you?"

Seeing he was having fun at her expense didn't keep her from being embarrassed. She blushed.

"That's okay, Sally. Just proves you're human."

That helped, and she went on. "I've toyed with the idea of going to Al-Anon. Heard of it?" He had. Margaret had suggested it too. From his wife, it came across as gratuitous. But coming from Sally, who broached it more like a friend than a professional, he took the possibility more seriously.

Maybe I am downplaying it, he thought. *This boy-named-Sue thing is getting old, wearing thin like a once-favorite white shirt with a fraying collar.* A few days later, he suddenly thought, *What the hell? I'll do it. I might learn something. But to heck with this Al-Anon thing, probably a bunch of people milking the victim thing for all they are worth. No, I want the real thing.*

He chose an AA chapter on the other side of town, where he probably wouldn't run into anybody he knew. He didn't mind the drive. He used a car service and sat in the back seat making calls.

The meeting was held in a basement room of a church. As he walked into the building and down the stairs, people nodded to him. He was struck right away by how the meeting started. They went around the room, all twenty-five or so of them, all men, and each person stated how long, in days, weeks, months, or years—or not at all—he'd been sober; every meeting started that way. When it was his turn that first night, everyone turning to look at him, he said, unapologetically, "My whole life." Except for some wondering looks, no one responded.

It was a strange feeling. *Exposed: that's it. Here I'm not a big shot. I'm not Father. I'm just another Joe Blow with a sad story.* He straightened his shoulders, stiffened his spine. He could handle it.

There was time that evening for several people to talk with blistering honesty about how they had bottomed out and how they were recovering or trying to. It wasn't until the next meeting that someone addressed him, an older, long-sober guy, although still, as he said, "recovering."

"Why are you here?" He was point-blank direct but not hostile.

"My father guzzled six-packs. Maybe I can learn something."

"Have a ball."

In meeting after meeting, they put people "in the barrel," attacked their illusions, their defenses. Mercifully, they left Sam alone. When he wasn't traveling, he kept attending, drawn to it like a book he couldn't put down.

The other side of life, he remarked to himself. But instead of feeling superior, he felt a kinship with the other men, not as strange as it might seem. Life had been a struggle for him too.

Three months into it, he was approached during a break by the veteran who had questioned him in group, his voice made raspy by cigarette smoke. Sam admired the way he'd enter late during someone's turn and cut to the crux. "You've got a sponsor now—me," he said. Sam couldn't make out whether that was meant as a gift or a threat. His cotton button-down shirt was wrinkled, his old jeans were wrinkled, and so was the skin on his face. In Sam's world, he'd start calling this unprepossessing guy "Wrinkles" on the spot. Why? To cut the guy down to size.

"Don't waste your time on me."

"Oh, yeah. What keeps you coming back here?"

Who does this guy think he is? Sam thought. He had come to accept Sally as a peer, but this man acted like he was in charge, had authority over Sam. Suddenly, the specter of his father darkened his mind, making him feel out of sorts. That threw him for a moment, but he did his best not to let it show. He summoned his considerable personal powers. He wasn't about to be intimidated by some stranger, however credible. Sam looked him in the eye and said, "Like I told you the last time you asked, I'm here to learn."

"Oh, yeah, what are you learning? Name one thing."

It had been many years since anyone treated him this way, but Sam stayed composed as he gathered his thoughts. "Life is a big struggle; I knew that but had no idea how much company I had." He paused, waiting for a reaction. There was none. "Here's what's new: A lot of the struggle is internal. You're fighting yourself."

"Not bad. Not bad for a rookie." The rough edge came off his voice, and he held out his hand. "I'm Gus." Sam already knew his name but appreciated the gesture.

They met on the following Saturday in a diner. Gus chose a booth off in the corner. It was clear from the way the waitress greeted him that he was a regular. They both ordered black coffee, nothing to eat. "Your father an alcoholic?" Gus asked.

"He drank a lot, but he wasn't an alcoholic." Gus asked for details and pounced.

"C'mon, mate! How many drunks have I seen drag their sad asses in here and claim they're not alcoholics? Your dad's shit stinks! Stop pretending it doesn't!"

It was like some 350-pound offensive lineman had knocked Sam to the ground. He sat there for a while, not offended. Gus sat quietly, as he often did. "I don't want to typecast him," Sam finally said.

"You mean you don't want to stigmatize him." Still direct as a hammer, a bit of compassion for the nail had crept in.

A month later, they met again on a Saturday, same place. "Where do you work?" Gus asked.

"Stellar."

"What do you do?" It felt like an interrogation. None of the rapport built up the last time carried over.

"I run a business."

"One of those higher-ups, huh?" Gus sneered. "What did your dad do?"

"Plumber."

"Blue-collar family, and look at you. Think you're hot shit, I bet!"

"No. Not at all." Sam bit off the words.

"More like the opposite?" Sam nodded, and Gus smiled knowingly. "You're just as easy to typecast as your father. 'The hero type,' not defeated by the circumstances, rose above it, way above it in this case. But, true to form, you still think you're a chump. Right?"

How can he be so sure? Sam thought, *I'm not sure.*

"Here you are, a big guy in the world, but you still feel small. Why? Why? Because your drunk father made you feel small, that's why! Got it?"

To Sam, it sounded too pat, yet it seemed to fit.

Sally Plays Catch-Up

In the four months Sam had been going to AA, he had canceled two of his monthly meetings with Sally, and she was getting a little uneasy. He had said nothing about AA on the theory that he'd surprise her if he got something out of it. Now he was itching to tell her. They were back in his office in their usual places on either side of the desk.

"My AA sponsor, Gus—," he began.

"You're going to AA!"

"Didn't I tell you?" He couldn't resist toying with her. "Anyway, he's rough-cut and untrained, but he's got wise eyes. You know, he may be as good at this stuff as you are." Tweaking her again made him merry.

But it didn't make her merry. Nor did she relish having another helper come on the scene. *I thought I was the one guiding him.* Distracted, she missed her cue to join him in their usual friendly combativeness as she sat there and sulked.

"What's got into you?" he said, taken aback and actually hurt. His face clouded over.

Oh no, I've lost him, she thought and had to fight hard to keep her face from crumpling. Presently, she pulled herself together and said, "Tell me, Sam."

"That guy was tough—I mean *tough.* Nothing I've seen since—" He stopped.

"Your father?" she said quietly.

"Speaking of him—" He took a deep breath. "He *was* an alcoholic; you were right. You didn't actually say that, but that's what you meant, right?" She nodded, and he went on. "No surprise, right? What you'd expect of AA, right? But *this* I didn't expect. Gus said"—Sally cringed at the name—"like a phoenix, I've risen from the ashes. Redemption. It's as if I'm saved."

"Okaaaay," she said, drawing out the word, struggling to follow. He waited.

"All of a sudden, you talk to some guy—" She wouldn't say his name; it stuck in her craw. "—and, suddenly, you're saved?" Her voice dripped with incredulity, not to mention disrespect.

"Wait a minute, Scrappy. I told you, that word, *saved,* goes way back." Nicknames like that were purely intuitive, but if pressed, he'd admit or discover they were terms of affection and terms of derision, the mix varying with the occasion.

"What do you mean? I don't remember that." Fear rippled through her. *What are you doing, Sally, getting into pitched battle with a client? Totally unprofessional.*

"That word, *saved,* it goes way back." A prayer from attending Mass flitted through his mind: "Help me, God my Savior, for the glory of Your name, deliver me and forgive me for my sins." A lapsed Catholic, he could still rattle off psalms, hymns, prayers, large chunks of the liturgy. "I told you my first supervisor saved me, literally. It was up or out, and without his help, I definitely would've been out in the cold. At the time, it was a fate worse than death."

In a much smaller voice she said, "Oh, now I remember. Sorry, Sam." She hung her head, abashed, embarrassed, mortified.

He waved away the apology. "This I didn't tell you: In the early days, when I was working myself to death, my mother on one of our regular calls said, 'Sam, it's like you're afraid you won't shape up.'"

"Shaped up—is that the same thing as saved?" she said mildly.

"Let's not split hairs. My mother was right. I was desperately trying to whip myself into shape."

"Like you whip organizations into shape?" It was coming together in her mind too. Like the two of them were again in a groove.

"Good point," he said, sounding upbeat. "Whip myself into shape by whipping organizations into shape."

"Great, you see it, Sam. But do you feel it?"

"Feel it?" He looked at his midriff as if he were consulting his feelings. "No."

"You know what they say: You can take the boy out of the jungle, but you can't take the jungle out of the boy. You can't stop feeling there's something wrong with you." He didn't object. "Does it have anything to do with your father?"

"Could be. He was a great one for depreciating my worth. Sally, I've got a lot to think about; I'll take it from here."

She missed that completely, actually didn't hear it at all. She was excited about something completely different: *Finally, the opening I've been waiting for.* She also felt a pressing need to redeem herself.

"You're catching up with yourself, right? And when you do, it will be a great feeling. But in the meantime, what about everyone else? What can you do to help other people feel good about themselves?" She was operating on the theory that we treat other people the way we treat ourselves. If Sam learned to make other people feel better about themselves, he'd feel better about himself and vice versa.

"By doing what?"

"Telling them 'Good job' when they do a good job," she said.

"Nope. A job done well is its own reward. But the point is I don't trust praise. It makes people complacent," he said.

Laughing, she said, "How would you know if you don't dispense it?"

He gave a little sideways smile; he didn't seem to mind being laughed at. "Fine. I'll think about that too. But did you hear what I said? I'll go it alone now."

It's Over

Now she heard him. "What—you're ending the engagement? But we've just gotten started." She was devastated. It was like her very reason for being had been snatched away. He nodded and seemed to be waiting for her to leave. Head down, she stuffed her papers and pad into her briefcase.

As she walked toward the door, he called out to her, "Sally, you've been a good sport. Thanks." High praise coming from him, but it didn't make a dent.

On her way out, she was relieved that she didn't run into anyone she knew. Outside, she leaned against the building, bricks poking into her, writhing with self-recrimination. She was sure her rank unprofessionalism had done it, had killed the assignment. Charlie, the GM, of all people, saw her and walked up.

"How's it going?" he asked, looking at her curiously.

"I thought fine but apparently not: Sam just ended the engagement."

"Permanently? I wouldn't assume that. I don't have to tell you his heart may be in the right place, but he's rough around the edges."

That night, Sam told his wife as they were passing each other on the stairs, "I've dropped her."

She scrunched her face in disbelief. "What??"

Pleased to get a rise out of her, he said, "Sally, the coach."

"I knew who you meant. But why would you do that?!"

"I've had enough for now." He hadn't said a word to Margaret about being redeemed. He was afraid of a letdown.

"It's your funeral," she said, turning away.

Sequel

A year went by without any contact except for an exchange of "Happy Holidays" cards. *At least I'm still on his list*, Sally thought, but it didn't relieve her severe pangs of guilt for screwing things up. Unknown to her, though, her idea of making other people feel good—with words, that is, actual words—had made an impression.

Sam's first stop was to his own daughter, Lisa, the one he gave a hard time to. He wrote her a little note (he had good penmanship) and placed it on her pillow after she'd left for school. When he got home from work that evening, she rushed up to him and threw her arms around his neck.

"Thank you, Daddy, thank you so much for your note."

He was astonished. He never dreamed a little note like that could mean so much. He hadn't heard her say *Daddy* for a very long time.

It took him a few weeks to decide on his next stop. Charlie, the GM who had followed Sam from assignment to assignment, had distinguished himself once again. Sam had asked Charlie to expedite the installation in Sam's division of a cross-business ERP system, AI-enabled software for integrating business processes. Often, it's a horror story. But Charlie had gotten it done on time and under budget. Enormously pleased, Sam thought he'd just come out and say so to Charlie. Normally, he'd let good work be its own reward—that plus a bump in comp.

Charlie walked into Sam's office and was surprised to see Sam sitting in an upholstered chair at the other end of his office. Wondering if Sam's wall was starting to come down, Charlie seated himself on the adjacent gray couch. "What's up?"

Sam cleared his throat, cleared it again, as if he were trying to cough up the words. Sweat broke out on his forehead. *What the hell*, he said to himself. Finally, he spoke: "The year's winding down, and I thought we could look ahead, informally, you know."

Charlie was mystified. Sam and the team had, according to the corporate calendar, already laid out the long-range plan and were soon due to firm up next year's budget. Sam kept the conversation going, but it went nowhere. Charlie walked out scratching his head: What was that about?

Acting on Sally's advice hadn't prompted Sam to contact her. A job offer did. Sally walked into his office only to find the big chair behind his desk empty. *He must have stepped out*, she thought.

"Over here," he called out.

Seeing him on the chair, and not in his fortified position, made her eyes go wide. She seated herself on the gray couch and said, "What's up?" She knew he liked to get straight to the point, but more than that, she was uneasy: *Why has he changed his mind?*

"Good to see you," he said, not answering her question. She leaned her head back as if to say, *Really, you're glad to see me?* "Yeah, you're really the only thought partner—about myself—I have ever had."

What about Gus? she thought but couldn't help being gratified it was her, not him.

"You'll come in handy now," he finished.

"Since when are you doling out feel-good?" She wasn't outright hostile, but now that she was back in his good graces, her stored-up resentment gushed out. *Watch it*, she instructed herself.

He pursed his lips but made no response to her snippy comment. Instead, he went ahead as planned. "I've been offered a CEO role, in another company." A rival company had approached him; their CEO was stepping down in a year. Sam would start as president and COO and take over in a year. They knew he was a turnaround type but didn't slot him. He could be counted on to get results; that's what mattered to them. With integrity.

At that big news, her mood instantly shifted. "You have! Congratulations! Will you take it?

"I'm sorely tempted."

"What does Margaret say?"

"Haven't told her. I never know what I'll get, a voice of reason or full-blast upset. I'll wait till I'm clear in my own mind."

"What can I do for you?"

"Check my motivation."

She was impressed and instantly got on the balls of her feet. "Okay, two questions. First, what attracts you to the job, the actual substance of it?"

"The chance, in that seat, to shape an entire company. Everything would be up for grabs: strategy, structure, the culture, staffing, innovation—everything. Very attractive."

He glowed in a way she'd never seen before. "I see the appeal. Second question: What does the job *represent* that attracts you?"

"You mean status, ego?" She did. "Well, I'd be lying if I said none of that. The role is the capstone of an executive's career. For me personally, it would be the ultimate vindication, no doubt about it. The money, as a measure of success—not so much. I have all I need."

"You check out; the job checks out. What's keeping you from taking it?"

"Not sure I want to go to war again."

That struck her. She'd never given much thought to what his big job took out of him.

"Better bring Margaret under the tent. Unless you want to commute."

"You're right. I'll keep you posted." He paused. "One other thing: I couldn't do it."

She had no idea what he meant, but the slight upturn of his lips told her he was once again having a little fun with her. "Oh?" she said, playing along.

He skipped over the note to Lisa and told her about his failed attempt to praise Charlie. "It would have taken a Heimlich maneuver to spit the words out," he said. "It was agonizing."

"That hard, really?" She didn't know whether to take him seriously. That hard, he repeated. She was shocked. Last time, he had seen the light, and that convinced her that he could do it, that he would do it. But he proved unable, and that meant she had failed, that she was incompetent. On a good day, it wouldn't have hit her so hard, but she was coming down with a cold, and her defenses were down too.

But it wasn't just that. She had pinned her hopes on this backdoor move: If he gave other people recognition, then he'd better recognize his own value; he'd place less emotional weight on what's wrong. And if the move came off, then she could declare her work with him a success.

"Knock, knock, anybody home?"

She shook her head twice attempting to clear it.

"What—are you giving up on me?" he said. It wasn't self-pity; it was friendly mockery.

She smiled ruefully. "Sorry, Sam, I'm off my game today."

"Don't worry about it." He went over to his desk and jotted something on a piece of paper, folded it neatly, and put it in a self-sealing envelope. Handing her the envelope, he said, "We'll stay in touch. In the meantime have a great life."

She stuffed it in her bag, didn't bother to thank him. Walking down the hall, she was still not herself, but she happened to see the sign for Charlie's office and stopped to say good-bye. He was there and jumped up to meet her. "You're a magician!"

"What?!" She was utterly bewildered.

"Yes, yes. I got this great note from Sam, thanking me for everything! In all these years, there's never been anything like it. I knew he thought highly of me, but this was different." She narrowed her eyes, trying to take it in. "Not just me, Sally. Other people around the office have been getting these kinds of notes. Truly, you've worked wonders. His wall's coming down."

In the car taking her to the airport, she leaned back and tried to catch her breath. It was as if she'd just staggered off a roller coaster. A few minutes later, she thought to open the envelope. *Now what could this be?*

"Dear Sally," it read, "there's a fallback; I'm surprised you didn't think of it. But I'm sure you will."

She looked up from the letter: *The devil, he's not* telling me! *But I outfoxed him: Someone else let me in on it.*

She read on: "Thanks for being such a good sport. And a big help; God knows I didn't make it easy. Working with you has meant more to me than you will ever know."

She glowed. *That Sam, he's something else.*

PROLOGUE

A senior manager who specializes in putting out business fires is combustible when he shouldn't be. Can he change enough to save his relationship with the love of his life? Can he stop fighting the need to reform?

FIGHT BREWING

It's never just one thing—a motive, a stance, a penchant—even if that one thing burns like wildfire.

"Can I come over?" he'd asked, mentioning something about a new venture he and his wife had undertaken.

"Good to see you," he said, shaking my hand energetically. He stuffed his scarf and hat into the sleeve of his overcoat and handed it to me.

Mid-January in New York, the sun had set discouragingly early, barely 4:30. Instantly, the sky went black, zero afterlight on the western horizon. I led him into the living room, lamps everywhere, all lit up. I motioned him to a wing chair and settled into its nearby twin.

On the phone, he'd told me he wanted to talk about a new venture, something to do with autism. Their daughter was on the spectrum but nothing serious. But here's how he began: "Michaela and I are spending a lot more time together. And, wonder of wonders, we've struck that spark again."

"Romantic?" I asked.

"Of course, but the thing is, Michaela's pleased with me. That's cause for celebration, right? How about some red wine?" I poured;

he twirled the glass around, made approving noises. Little blue veins ran along his nostrils. "I overindulge," he once told me. "I fly into excess." I couldn't tell if he was confessing or bragging.

"Now, when I feel really bad about myself, I know Michaela can help," he continued.

"She's a safe haven?"

"Base camp," he said.

"Nothing more *bas*ic?" I asked, accentuating the pun.

He laughed. "All along, it's been there for the taking, her fondness for me, but I get worked up. That's what I'm afraid of. It's back, but I'll spoil it," he said.

"I'll never forget that scene at the airline counter." He had made a spectacle of himself. I felt sorry for his wife and three kids.

"Yeah, I really let the ticket agent have it," he said.

"She had no idea who she was dealing with," I said, colluding a bit. "What got into you?"

"Her attitude stunk, stunk to the high heavens," he said.

"I didn't care for it myself; that was on her. But aren't we responsible for our reactions?"

He shrugged.

"How deeply do you want to get into this?" I said.

"Do we know any other way?" he said.

"I like your attitude! So, with Michaela, what gets into you?" I asked. There had been a time when I'd advised him on leading, on living. At this stage, I regarded us as friends. He opened up like a flag unfurling.

"She says I'm defensive," he said. "If I can't convince her of something, she'll say, 'Let's move on.' But I press the point. Finally, she can't stand it any longer, and she'll run into the bedroom, slamming the door behind her. At my worst, I run after her and shout through the door, which is locked."

He looked at me.

"No, I'm not proud of it," he said. "Yes, I feel terrible later." He looked away and shifted in his chair, then turned back to me, glaring.

"Listen. My father was a fighter too," he said. "He grew up in a rough place. All the neighborhood kids fought with their fists. That's the vision of life he drilled into me: 'Hit back; hit back harder.' So, you see, it's not my fault I'm this way."

"It's preordained?" I asked.

"I'm definitely my father's son. In ninth grade, I went to a new school and three tenth graders ganged up on me in an empty gymnasium. I didn't cry. I didn't report them to the principal. Nope. I caught up with those kids one at a time and beat them up."

"Tough kid. But where are you going with this?" I asked.

"Here's where: I'd like to punch out my boss, the COO. He's so damned full of himself. What an asshole," he said.

"That's your private opinion?"

"Hell, no. I broadcast it. I want to tarnish his ego," he said.

"What if you're tarnishing your own reputation?"

"Couldn't care less," he said.

His cavalier attitude was getting to me. "What's it to you anyway—that the COO's like that?"

He shifted in his chair again. "I have to work for him."

"You've never worked for an a-hole before?"

He rolled his eyes, but I wanted a real answer.

"You're risking your job acting like that," I said. "Seriously, why do you care so much?"

He closed his eyes for a moment. "The real truth: I'm just an object to him, not a human being."

I asked him what that felt like. He walked over to the window. "That grassy area across the street with the benches around it— ever go over there?" The answer was yes. He sat down again. "I don't know. I can't come up with anything. Let's see: What would Michaela say? She'd say, 'Your feelings are hurt.'"

"Nice footwork. There's an implication—," I said.

"What—that other people have feelings too?" His eyes smiled but a moment later lost their light. "Are you trying to take the fight out of me? Because my career would have gone nowhere without it."

"Tell me."

"People called me 'the fireman,'" he said. "You want an example? Here's one." He hit the coffee table with his fist. "I was handed a piece-of-crap imaging business; a next-gen imaging device had been rushed to market. By the guy before me. There were serious quality issues, which he downplayed." He stood up and sat right down again.

"What did I do?" He continued and pounded the table again. "I flew to a bunch of places to hear from customers directly. And I did a deep dive with the technical people. All that took three months. My going-in hunch was right: The product had to be pulled from the market. It was a really painful decision, because it meant pissing off customers and losing a lot of money, and it meant laying off a bunch of people in sales and in tech services, which I hated to do." He started to stand up again but didn't.

"The device had to be redesigned from the ground up. My boss went along with the decision but imposed a super aggressive time-line. So aggressive that several people ended up in the hospital; not me, fortunately. But we met the deadline."

"Heroics!" I said, impressed.

"You say heroics; I say luck."

"You're kidding."

"I mean it. I'm just a little boat swept along by the Big Muddy," he said.

"Do you ever take credit for anything?"

"Well, there was one time," he said. "The morning of the 9/11 attacks, I was on the West Coast and scheduled to fly back that day to Boston, where we lived at the time. The possibility of being stranded out west for days freaked me out. I knew flights on the East Coast would be canceled, so I flew to Atlanta, rented a car, and drove home from there. That, I give myself credit for. Otherwise, it's luck."

"When it's not luck, what is it then?"

"Oh, that's passion. Passion to get it right," he said.

"That passion of yours, it burns hot."

"How else does anything get done?!" he said. "Anything difficult, I mean."

"I agree. But what about when your passion heats up like water brought to a boil?"

"Part of me disapproves," he said. "That guy sits here." He pointed to his left shoulder.

"That guy, who is he?" I asked.

"Reason, I suppose."

"Ah, reason as opposed to emotion. Which is stronger?"

"Reason is a little guy. A weakling," he said. His voice dripped with contempt. "Doesn't stand a chance."

"Yeah, I'm getting that impression," I said with faint sarcasm that I immediately regretted.

"What's the message? Be nice to the meek because they'll inherit the Earth?" he said.

"Wouldn't it be good to have an off switch when passion turns ugly?"

"Don't get the wrong impression. There are little promising signs, like the crocuses that will soon poke up in Central Park," he said.

"Case in point: Michaela?"

"How d'ya know? You see, I never suspect Michaela will hurt me. She might, but I never suspect she will."

"You trust her?"

"Completely. With Michaela, my guard is down," he said.

"What's that worth?"

"It means the world to me." He looked away for a few moments, then held out his glass.

I took it, filled it, and handed it over.

Glass back in hand, he looked askance at me. "Are you trying to domesticate me?"

"Do you really think I've got that up my sleeve?" I said.

He thought for a moment. "No, not really. But this touchy-feely stuff is getting to me."

"Let's say you tried to purge your fighting spirit, set a goal to do that. What are your chances?"

"Good point. No chance. But what if it's innate?"

"Then you can't be blamed for it," I said. "But isn't it on the grown person to deal with their inbred tendencies?"

"I suppose, but the leopard can't change its spots."

"The leopard, no. But an adult can outgrow their worst tendencies," I said.

He looked doubtful.

"More to the point, where do you come out on all of this?"

"There's a parable—Cherokee, supposedly," he began. "The Cherokee were great warriors, which, unfortunately, didn't save them from being evicted from their native lands. They were overmatched. But the parable, it stars two wolves. One of them selfish, envious, pessimistic, wicked, dark. The other one filled with light, compassion, optimism, generosity of spirit. The one who wins is whichever one you feed."

"So?" I wanted him to say the good wolf.

"I feed them both."

"Why am I not surprised?" I said.

He looked down at his watch. "Hey, it's past your bedtime."

"Wait. If I were a betting man—"

"Keep your money in your pocket," he said, interrupting, smiling impishly. "With me, there's always a fight brewing. As if you didn't know."

I retrieved his coat and hoisted it up to his shoulders as he dug his arms in. Opening the apartment door himself, he stepped into the elevator vestibule.

"A parting thought," I said. "Badmouthing people is beneath you."

"What do you mean, 'beneath me'?"

"Beneath your dignity," I said.

"What dignity?"

His Manifesto

Ten days later, we met again, this time at Starbucks, the one at the corner of 3rd Avenue and 65th. I secluded us in the little nook in the back. That day, the sun actually had some warmth to it. He had another appointment, so he got right down to it, none of the usual wit and mischief.

"I talked it over with Michaela," he said, "and here's where I come out. Six things. One: There's a big difference between the guy I thought I was and the guy I actually am."

"That's big," I said. I wasn't expecting anything nearly as sweeping as that."

"Wait; there's more." He was friendly but intent. "Two: I've met the enemy, and the enemy is me."

"Do you actually mean that? Did Michaela give you truth serum?"

He just smiled. "Three: the bad guy isn't the COO. The bad guy is me. Four: Just like me, other people need to be respected."

"You're serious?" I said. "You're not pulling my leg?"

"What do you take me for?" he said, grinning. "Five: You're right; badmouthing is beneath me. Six: Reason, that ninety-pound weakling—like I said, it can't stand up to passion, doesn't have a prayer—"

"Yeah, especially when passion turns hostile and dark," I interrupted.

"Correct, but listen to this: Wisdom can." He pointed to his left shoulder. "Wisdom is canny. It's savvy. Wisdom is powerful."

"Rarely has the world seen a change of heart like this," I said.

"Want proof? Just the other day, a cab driver was rude to us. Normally, I'd jump down the guy's throat. But I just sat back and took Michaela's hand. That always calms me down. So you see, there's hope."

"Yes, I see." It pleased me he'd decided to straighten up and fly right, as my father instructed me to do.

"Look," he said brightly. "It's right here on my pen." The lettering was high design and hard to make out. Pointing with his index finger, he deciphered the words for me one phrase at a time: "'The pen . . . is mightier . . . than the sword.'"

"Nifty," I said.

It was time for him to go. As we put on our outer garments, he said, "Oh, I just came up with a seventh: A tipsy me is no good for anybody."

Their Next Encounter

It was three months before we got together again. I returned his call and a female voice answered.

"Could this be Michaela?" I asked.

"None other," she answered charmingly. "Who might this be?" I told her. "Oh, I'm very pleased to meet you. But it's not me you're calling. I'll get him." She was polished marble to his rough granite.

He and I met again in the apartment. Still February, a biting cold night, frost slowly creeping across the windows like vines, obscuring the view. I greeted him heartily as he walked in. No question I was buoyed by his big breakthrough.

"Good to see you," he said, and I thought I detected a certain lack of gusto. "Before we get into it, I've got to tell you about our trip to Japan." He enthused for a few minutes about the nation's ultramodern trains that actually run on time. "But you can also experience ancient Japanese customs firsthand."

"Say, did you visit the atomic bomb memorial in Hiroshima?" I asked, joining him for the moment.

"We did. Strikingly beautiful and very moving. Some tourists avoid it."

"Yeah, well, civilization isn't always civil, is it? So how's it going?" I asked, trying to get him on track.

"Well, let me first update you on our autism effort," he said.

I was getting impatient but sat on it.

"Michaela and I have decided to go after the root cause. None of this symptomatic stuff—help people cope better with a bad situation. We'll see what can be done with gene-splitting tools like CRISPR to relieve the condition itself."

"You wouldn't be avoiding the subject, would you?"

"What subject?" he said, playing innocent.

"You know what I mean. Where we left off last time." I had a sinking feeling.

"How about some red wine? Is there an open bottle?"

I felt like resisting but went along. "This one's from Sicily," I said, glass in hand. "The guy at the wine store called it 'rebellious.'"

He took a sip. "Earthy with a definite tannic edge." Then he downed the rest. "Bring the bottle. I can pour it myself."

"That's okay. I'll do the honors."

He shot forward in the chair. "Are you trying to manage me?"

He wasn't wrong. There was no way I was going to help him get sloppy drunk in my place. "Take it easy," I said calmly.

"You're so damn steady."

Uh-oh, I thought. *This is what I get for mixing social and professional.* "Yeah, yeah. What's up? You can just come out and say it."

"I have my doubts about this make-me-a-better-person bit," he said.

"My head's spinning. What happened to your six-point manifesto? Seven-point."

"Well, I hadn't actually committed, right?"

I laughed. "Got me on technicalities." I could have sworn he blushed. "You might as well tell me what's going on."

He came out with it. "I backslid." It wasn't he who had taken me in; I had taken myself in. Maybe it was my native optimism—or just plain naivete.

"Want to know what happened? I acted up with none other than the—?" He left a blank for me to fill in.

"The COO." I guessed right. Although he'd met last year's annual objectives, he had been graded down for bad behavior. That had never happened before. But what got to him was that his bonus was docked by 25 percent.

"Act it out for me, would you?" I said. "I'm the COO."

He hesitated. "This is awkward." He stood over me and raised his voice. 'This is the thanks I get! Well, screw you and the horse you rode in on.'"

I motioned him away. "You're invading my space."

"What, can't take it?" His face was red.

I made a time-out sign, signaling the end of the role-play. "Was that an exact replica?" I asked.

He sat back down. "Exaggerated. I didn't get in his face like that."

"Tell me something. Do you get a charge out of being pissed off?"

"Come to think of it, I do. I'm never more fully alive than when I get royally pissed off. It's like all my nerve endings stand on end, erect, if you know what I mean."

"Pyrotechnics turn you on?" I asked.

"Of course; I'm a fireman, remember? But I light fires too." He turned thoughtful; I could see it in his eyes. "Yeah, that's the problem."

"That crossed my mind too. I'm glad you thought of it." I walked over to the window. "It's gotten heated in here—know what I mean?" I said. "Let's go toss the football. That grassy space across the street is lit."

"That's crazy," he said, but he got to his feet.

I dug the ball out of the hall closet. No coats. He threw a tight spiral. No wonder he played quarterback in high school. His bullet passes slammed into my gut.

"Hey," I shouted after he'd whipped a few at me, "not so hard."

He smiled and took something off the ball. Having done enough to begin to get winded, we took the elevator back up.

"Great idea," he said and punched me on the shoulder.

"Still need that wine?" I asked.

He shook his head no. "You haven't heard the worst yet." His tone was grave, funereal. "After that bust of a meeting with my boss," he said, "I went home and promptly took it out on Michaela. At the slightest pretext. She was shocked and left the room right away; this time, I let her be. But I did tiptoe over to the door, and I could hear her sobbing. Hours later, when she emerged from the room, I apologized, but it didn't register. She was back in her shell. The lights had gone out."

"Really sorry to hear that," I said.

"Not as sorry as I am," he said. "I'll go now. What else is there to say?"

Aftermath of the Firestorms

A week later, I called to see how he was doing. "My boss seems to have forgiven me. He told me, 'You need a filter.' Boy, do I. Can I come over?"

"Okay, but I've got a hard stop at noon."

When the doorbell rang, he was standing there with a dripping umbrella. I hadn't noticed the rain start. Apartments in New York, the older ones, are like caves; you're sealed off from the weather. I stuck the umbrella in the umbrella stand and shook off his coat there, on the tile floor, before hanging it in the foyer closet. He took the same wing chair.

"Okay. Michaela. I've tried to strike that spark again, but it's like rubbing two sticks together to start a fire. Nothing happens except pieces of bark fall off. I'll never win her back."

"You've won her back before," I said.

He smirked. "Too many times to count. What do I do with the big bad wolf?"

"You could put it on a leash," I said.

"Right, like some dog. Besides, the big bad wolf is a lot of fun. Look, I like to get drunk. I was dancing wildly with a friend's wife at our New Year's Eve party, and I toppled over."

"Which is it—the wolf's aggressive, or the wolf's intoxicated?"

"The big bad wolf is out of control," he said.

"Why didn't I think of that? For the sake of argument, at the other end of that leash is—"

"Maturity," he said. First it was wisdom, now maturity.

I didn't quibble.

"But maturity is boring."

"You're incorrigible!" I said, laughing. "Here's a question: What's lost now, between you and Michaela?"

"Peace. During our early-on halcyon days, we dropped our swords and shields—well, my sword and her shield."

"Here's a thought that just came to me," I said. "Michaela's been a safe haven, right?"

He nodded.

"But are you a safe haven for her?"

"Never thought of it." It sounded like he wanted to punch some-body. But a moment later, his voice collapsed into sadness. "No, it never once crossed my mind."

His hand on the doorknob, he looked back. "I always thought I was a good provider—food, clothing, shelter. But one necessity of life was missing from the list. I damn well better add it."

A week later, he called. "So far, so good. But I didn't breathe a word of it to Michaela. Don't talk of love; show it, I told myself." A month later, he called again. "Still on course. The new news: I've sworn off alcohol in any form. A sober me is a better me."

Hearing Directly from Michaela

Several months went by. I wanted to believe it was going well, but I was afraid it wasn't. Finally, he called. He wanted me to talk with Michaela. She was willing if I was.

She and I met one morning in the restaurant at the Carlyle, where people talk in hushed tones, and the coffee, brought to the table in a French press, is served in fine china. She had taught high school math in the public schools—in Williamsburg, before it was gentrified.

"It was rewarding, but after twenty years, I felt I had done my bit for society and retired," she said. "Since then, I've volunteered, gone to the theater Wednesday afternoon, when you can get half-price tickets, joined a daytime book club. But what I've been up to is not why he wanted us to talk."

"Why does he want us to talk?" I asked.

"He didn't say, but, probably, he wants me to give you a good report, that now he treats me like a precious Fabergé egg." She took a sip of coffee. "It's strong prepared this way. But I don't want to give you the wrong impression. He is a little better."

"Do you think there's been a change of heart?"

She poured a little cream and stirred it with a little silver spoon. "I'll say this much: It does seem like his heart is in the right place.

I'm not saying we're now living in an ideal climate, Laguna Beach or something. But there are fewer storms. I'll take it. I'd be a fool not to."

"You saw the realizations he wrote up a couple months back?" I asked.

"Oh, sure. I helped him with that. It was a sort of constitution. 'We the people, in order to form a more perfect union.'"

"Do you think the change, to the extent he has made one, is real?"

"It's certainly not faked," she said. "But if you're asking if it will last, who knows? Do you know?"

"I'm the last one to ask."

"Has he told you the latest at work?"

I indicated no.

"He's been taken out of the running for a top job. Maybe that's added to his incentive to be a success with me. I don't mean to be cynical." She took a sip of coffee. "You haven't asked me what his 'storms' were like."

"I wondered, of course, but I wasn't about to ask you. Boundaries, you know."

"Well, I'll tell you. At those times, I wasn't so much hurt and indignant as lonely—terribly lonely."

"That never occurred to me," I said.

She had an open face, smiled easily. I'd half expected her to be beaten down, but she wasn't. Hard-bitten? Maybe. I just hoped he would give her a reason to smile.

He called soon after the session had ended. "What did Michaela say?"

"I'd love to tell you, but I can't speak for her."

He understood.

"Why don't you ask her?"

"Yeah, why don't I?" he said.

An hour later, the phone rang. "She said it's far short of the ideal, but it's not as bad as it was. And if I behave myself, she might could make a place for me in her heart. She said that's what she told you."

Betraying nothing, I said, "That's not what you were hoping for."

"No, but I'll take it."

PROLOGUE

Credit to EmmaJean for rising above her childhood circumstances, but the emotional scars haven't disappeared, and, below awareness, they drag her down as a leader, as a mother, and as a spouse.

COMING IN FROM THE RAIN

E mmaJean, a rising star but not untarnished, sat across the table from Sanford, a middle-aged man who called himself a guide. It had been suggested to her that she spruce up her leadership, and she had chosen to work with him.

"How are you?" he asked.

"Fine," she said. That's what she told her husband every morning: "Fine."

Her husband, Dan, had learned to ask, "Fine-plus, fine-minus, or just plain fine?"

Typically, on that multiple-choice question, she tested well.

Today, she was anything but fine. Her performance appraisal was coming up, and she was panic stricken. *Shall I tell him?!* The truth, like the juice in an overripe nectarine, wanted out, but the skin was too thick.

"How about jotting down ten answers to the question: Who am I? Just a word or two for each."

A standard exercise. He slid a three-by-five card toward her.

"I'm a very private person," she said.

"Our discussions are confidential, as I mentioned. No back door to management." He had an impulse to throw in, "Cross my heart and hope to die." He wondered, *Is that her issue—trust? Let's see if she can learn to trust me.*

She dashed off her answers. When she held the card out to him, he said, "That's yours to keep. If you'd just read what you wrote."

She took a deep breath. "Okay, who am I? A woman, a careerist, mother, spouse, athlete, small-town girl, West Virginian by birth, baby in the family, achiever, introvert. How's that?"

"That's great. Care to put a little flesh on the bones?"

Lips sealed, she shook her head no.

"Maybe another time."

He was put in mind of oysters on a bed of ice waiting to be shucked. "That's fine, just fine," he said, making a show of respecting her limits. "But can I ask you a hypothetical question?" Now he was asking if he could ask.

"Okay."

"Good. If an up-and-coming woman is smarter than she thinks, how would that play out?"

"Um, she'd shy away, maybe not speak up when she had something to say. Not live up to her potential? That ain't me, if you're wondering. I'm gangbusters no matter what the weather. My husband says, 'You're going out in this?'"

"Got it," he said. Noting she had actually volunteered something about herself, he decided to chance it. "I could be wrong: You seem troubled."

"You're not wrong. I'm scared out of my wits I'll get fired." She worked for a company that made personal care products—skin cream, skin cleanser, lanolin soap, toothpaste, detergent, you name it. A few years ago, she was made head of the Andean region— Argentina, Chile, and Peru. The business was troubled. There was a good chance she, as a first-time general manager, would be in over her head. But it helped that marketing, the function she knew best, reigned supreme in the company. Just the advertising budget was fully six percent of sales. It also helped that she was fluent in Spanish, thanks to her husband's lineage. His parents had emigrated from Colombia. She and her husband were raising their kids bilingual; that meant so was she. Improbably, she was granted permission to stay in Chicago, not relocate to the company's regional office for Latin America in Miami.

"Why would you worry about getting fired?"

"That's nothing new. I've always worried about getting fired. But this year, I've got good reason for it. I didn't make a plan."

"This year. How about past years?"

"That was then, and this is now. I will say that, when I took over four years ago, the business was the black sheep of the company. Here's what we did, my team and I: Number one: We sorted out the portfolio of products and dropped 300 of the 800 SKUs. That allowed us to pump a lot more advertising money into the better-selling products. Two: We went after production delays. Rationalizing the portfolio helped a lot with that. Three: We shed subpar people. Then it was all about execution, grinding it out."

"And?" Sanford asked.

"The region had been losing two to four percent per year. The year before last, we delivered seven percent."

"Wouldn't your boss factor this in, the turnaround?"

"Why would he?"

Taking a flyer, he asked, "Has anyone ever told you you're better than you think?"

"My husband."

"Your husband believes in you?"

"He does, as a careerist anyway."

"Then what if, in fact, you are better than you think?"

"Unthinkable."

Dan, the Nurturing Husband

As much as her husband, Dan, believed in her, the weather of their marital life had never truly been fine. For one thing, she was reserved; she held back, even when they had sex, the ultimate intimate act. He could tell—she wasn't his first lover—but it didn't occur to him to object. He was the sort who settled for less. That quality was probably partly why, consciously or not, she'd chosen him in the first place. It made it easier for her to have her way.

Dan had quit his job when she was made head of the Andean region. Someone had to hold down the fort. It made sense financially too. His pay as a legal aid lawyer barely covered the cost of the nanny. At first, he had made little snippy comments like, "My big-shot wife." But before long, he discovered the upside. The unwelcome void in Dan's life turned into a chance to enjoy his kids and to help out if needed, but the upside for Dan had another side for EmmaJean.

One Saturday morning, EmmaJean and Dan were sitting on the

front porch drinking cappuccinos, and she thought to ask him how it was going.

"Have you noticed Ricky is off of math?" he said.

"No. How can you tell?"

"He usually does his math homework first, races through it. But then he started doing it last and dawdling over it. He was falling behind."

"Whatever that's about, it needs to be fixed, right away," she said, shifting instantly into problem-solving mode. "What do you think we should do?"

"Actually, it is pretty much fixed." Dan told her that after school one day, he and his son had sat together on the front porch while Ricky had his after-school grilled-cheese sandwich, which he made himself.

"Don't you like math anymore?" Dan had asked.

After a curt "No," Dan coaxed out the reason. Ricky's friend, Samuel, was doing better than he was, and Ricky had given up. Starting that evening, Dan sat with Ricky while he did his math homework.

"I only stepped in when Ricky got stuck. He just needed some support. By the end of the week, he'd caught up." Dan smiled.

"That's good,'" EmmaJean said, a beat too late.

She could have viewed Dan's success that day as hers too. Instead, she felt negated as a mother. Rather than enjoy the accomplishments of her husband and son, she only tasted misery. Clearly hearing the hesitation in her tone, Dan held back from telling her that their twelve-year-old daughter Melissa had started confiding in him.

EmmaJean waited until the morning of the performance appraisal to mention it to Dan. Distress was written all over her face. He was pained but, per usual, he took his cues from her and gave her a big hug and said nothing. Grateful, she kissed him on the cheek.

The appraisal was at noon, which spared her driving into Chicago during rush hour. Cedric, the head of International, had been her manager for a little less than a year. She was prepared for the worst. Panicky, she reached into her purse and gulped down half a Xanax moments before he arrived.

Looking serious, Cedric got right down to it. "You didn't meet your growth objectives for the year," he said.

Oh no, he's going to lower the boom, she thought.

"Volume was just sixty percent of plan. Terrible. Would you agree?"

At the word *terrible*, she caved in emotionally and gasped for breath.

He pulled up short. "Wait, I was kidding!"

"Kidding! What do you mean, kidding?" asked EmmaJean.

"Given the market conditions—the steep drop-off of demand— you've had a good year."

"But I didn't make plan."

"You did what could be done. Sharply reduced costs without cutting to the bone. The business won't be handicapped when demand goes back up. I give you a lot of credit."

She almost fell out of her chair. "I was expecting blame, not praise."

"Then you're almost certainly not expecting this: You're getting promoted."

Again, she gasped.

"To the head of LATAM," he added.

She flew to her feet. "Is this another joke?"

He rose to his feet too. "I kid you not."

"I'm sorry. I know I should be happy," said EmmaJean.

"That's okay. But may I say congratulations? It's well deserved."

Just days later, still swollen with feeling, she met with Sanford.

"Is something wrong?" he said out loud and thought, *What now?*

"I'm getting promoted. An office in the new tower on Michigan Avenue."

"And that's bad?" he asked, his tone light.

"Certain things about my past stick in my mind like a sliver, a nail in my foot." She flashed to an image of herself standing in the rain, statue-like, her face immobile. With the rain running down her face, you couldn't tell she was crying. Girls at school, a little clique, picked on her, delighted in it. She'd never let her face betray a thing. A clap of thunder brought her mother to the door. "Are you crazy?" her mother shouted.

She kept the thought to herself. To Sanford, she said, "I thought I might go to college. I would have been the first person in my whole family to do it. But my guidance counselor talked me out of it. 'You're not college material,' she told me."

"But here you are," Sanford said, "vaulted to a high floor in corporate headquarters. Once a caterpillar, now a butterfly."

"Me, a butterfly?" But he'd gotten her to laugh. "Only if I'm really management material. I don't even feel like I can tell Dan. The promotion isn't official anyway."

"Tell your husband," Sanford told her.

She finally got around to it when the two of them were cleaning up from Sunday brunch. He was excited. "The executive level: that means a big jump in salary, stock grants too. Now we can move to Oak Park!" He longed to live in a Frank Lloyd Wright house; there were several in that neighborhood.

"What's wrong with this house?" She was dead set against the outlay of capital and the added expense of a big house and a big yard.

But he kept trying to persuade her. "What's money for, EmmaJean? We've got plenty socked away, almost enough for you to retire. And, hey, I'm home all the time." It was as passionate as he ever got. But to her, their savings could vanish in an instant. He got nowhere but knew how to eat disappointment.

"My husband thinks we're upper class now," she told Sanford, exaggerating. "But I can still picture my father's blackened face, like some ghoulish Halloween mask, when he got back from the coal mine. My father was out sick a lot. Turned out it was black lung disease. Never enough to eat; we were evicted two or three times."

"To this day, you're holding on for dear life?" asked Sanford.

"Something like that."

Sanford thought for a moment. "Do you think your kids feel that way?"

"God, I hope not. I don't know why they would."

EmmaJean cared deeply about her kids; she left no doubt in their minds about that. She had trained them, like the pet dog they didn't have, to come running when she got home. She'd smother them with kisses: "Oh, honey, it's so good to see you, I love you so much." *Laying it on thick*, Dan thought, but kept it to himself.

Knowing no other way, her children had gone along with

EmmaJean's overzealous displays of showing her love until, one day, her twelve-year-old, Melissa, did not come running. EmmaJean called out for her.

Finally, she came trooping down the stairs. "I was doing my homework," her daughter explained. That sounded plausible. But when EmmaJean tried to smooch each cheek, Melissa pulled away. "Oh, Mom."

"What is it?" EmmaJean said, puzzled.

"Nothing. Just that it's—I don't know. Talk to Dad; he'll explain."

EmmaJean was shocked. Her trust in him was strong but not impervious to doubt.

That evening, EmmaJean went upstairs to read to the kids and tuck them in, Ricky first. To EmmaJean's relief, bedtime with Melissa came off as usual.

She found Dan in the living room reading a magazine. He made room for her on the couch, but she remained standing. "What's going on?" she demanded.

Dan crossed his arms. "What do you mean?"

"Are you and Melissa conspiring against me?"

Not knowing about the incident at the front door, Dan leapt to his feet. "What are you talking about?" His integrity was a cherished possession, and he was not about to have it impugned.

From the top of the stairs, Melissa called down in a quavering voice, "Is everything okay?"

"I'll take care of it," Dan said and ran upstairs.

That only added to EmmaJean's upset. She was the one who attended to the kids' nighttime needs. *He's up to something. The one person in the world I thought I could trust, and now this. How could*

he team up with one of the kids against me? How could he betray me?
When she heard him coming down the stairs, she jumped up, fire
in her eyes.

He raised his hands, saying. "Hold it, will you please? I can
explain." Melissa had told him what happened at the front door.

"It better be good." At his urging, they sat down. "Okay, I'm
waiting."

"She thinks you still treat her like a child."

"What's that supposed to mean?"

"Look, this is no reflection on you," he said, knowing full well it
was. "Melissa's growing up; that's all."

"What—I can't kiss her anymore?"

"Of course you can. Just cool it a little," he said.

Another woman might have dissolved in tears, but that was not
her way.

"Come over here," Dan said affectionately.

They hugged and went upstairs to bed. But she couldn't shake
the sense that she was a bad mother.

The next night at bedtime, EmmaJean told Melissa, "Dad and
I talked."

"Did you make up?"

"Yes."

Melissa scooted over to make room for her mother. "I get it,
Melissa. You're growing up—"

"Yes, Mom, I am. Let's read."

They did, but it was awkward. To be uncomfortable with her own
children was more than she could bear. They were her only refuge. *I
can't show affection to my own children? Where does that leave me?*

The Winds of Change

At work, rumors that the company might be acquired were buzzing around like deerflies, that unpleasant. EmmaJean assumed the potential acquirer was another company in the space, just bigger. But the reality was different. With the board's approval, the CEO and a small group of executives had struck a deal with a private-equity firm. Sequoia Capital had bought up forty percent of the company's publicly traded shares.

Along with the rest of senior management, EmmaJean was summoned to a meeting. In the front of the room, the CEO sat beside a stranger soon introduced as the PE firm's deal partner. He'd serve as chairman of the new entity. EmmaJean didn't know much about PE firms, but her distrust meter oscillated wildly. She began to sweat and was seized by an overpowering urge to run from the room.

Afterward, she was first to meet with Cedric. To settle her nerves, she had popped a Xanax, a whole pill. Cotton balls filled her head. "It's a whole new ball game, EmmaJean," her manager said neutrally, as hard to read as ever.

"What if I don't want to play?" It leapt out of her mouth, startling her as well as him.

"Look," he said, with a twisted smile. "I'm in the same boat."

Ah, he's not one of them. She softened. "These PE firms—I've heard, read horror stories about them," she said scornfully. "They cut costs to the bone. They leave the company in a weakened condition—bankrupt, often."

"Don't tar them all with the same brush."

"But what about the 'little people,' as the private equity guy called them? I come from a family of so-called little people—very little."

"That's just an unfortunate expression," Cedric said.

"That may be, but those money people, I don't trust them as far as I can throw them."

She faced the hateful task of breaking the news to her team and flew to Santiago to do it. She had gone there so often that the hotel stored her stuff between trips. Assembled there were the three country heads, as well as the CFO and the head of HR. She addressed them in Spanish.

"You've seen the announcement. I'm here to tell you what it means for us, to the extent that that's knowable now." She'd done her homework. "Frankly, I feared the worst. But as private equity firms go, this one—evidently, but we'll see—is not among the worst of the bunch, meaning they won't just cut, cut, cut, to maximize their internal rate of return. They claim they gain if the company gains."

"What does that mean for the rank and file?" asked the country manager of Peru.

"Supposedly, they won't demand wanton across-the-board cuts. But nothing's sacred."

If It's Not One Thing, It's a Mother

The following week, she got a rare call from her mother, who wanted to visit. *Nosy bitch*, EmmaJean said to herself. She and her mother hadn't seen each other since her father's funeral several years ago. Her mother had accosted her: "What's wrong with you, EmmaJean? You're not crying."

The morning her mother was due to arrive from West Virginia was sunny. EmmaJean actually found herself thinking, *Maybe, just maybe, this visit will go well.* But the sky had clouded over by the time her mother pulled into the driveway in her subcompact rental. There was no way EmmaJean was going to pick her up at O'Hare.

EmmaJean, along with her daughter and son, went out to meet her. When mother dearest stepped out of the car, the first thing out of her mother's mouth was, "Oh, EmmaJean, how pretty Melissa has gotten to be. How is that possible? You're not."

EmmaJean's sister, Jolene, is prettier than her and now her daughter. After a split-second delay—EmmaJean was out of practice—her defenses kicked in and walled off the stabbing pain. EmmaJean turned on her heel and marched double-time up the walk and into the house, leaving her mother's bags in the trunk. Inside, she leaned against the storm door, fuming. *Why does my mother's crap still get to me?*

Still angry, she brought it up with Sanford a few days later.

"How far back does that go?" he asked.

"What do you think?" she said, chafed at the lack of a sympathetic ear.

He bore her displeasure. "You really did have a hard start in life."

"My father was a lot worse, absolutely," she said.

"But you weren't defeated by it. There must have been offsets."

"You're right. My grandparents on my mother's side were a saving grace." EmmaJean was their youngest grandchild, and they doted on her. Her grandpa had retired from a skilled job at the local nylon intermediates plant, where he had been a union steward. Starting when she was twelve, he'd let her drive the old pickup truck by herself on their dirt driveway. On their long walks in the nearby hills, he pointed out the local flora and fauna. He taught her how to catch trout in the clear mountain stream, how to make the lures by hand, how to filet what she caught. From her granny, she learned to sauté the fish, a delicate art.

"They loved me, and they believed in me. I miss them terribly." She could cry.

By plan, EmmaJean and Sanford had gone off-site to delve into her leadership. They met at a hotel that also served as a conference center. He had recommended a day and the next morning. A better chance for deep learning, he had told her.

Deep, oh great, she thought.

When she walked into the conference room, he offered her the seat at the end of the antique mahogany table. She demurred, but he charmed her into taking it, all wordlessly.

Sanford began, "It's like we're marooned here at the corner of this very long boardroom table. But this is a retreat. We're meant to be on an island, an island in time, aren't we? Seat belt fastened?"

"Yup." She was apprehensive but kept it to herself.

"You're such a capable person. Consistently get good results through people in the right way. The very definition of good leadership." He paused for her to respond.

"That may be, but I know I'm no exemplar. Every single thing I'm good at, I know somebody who, in that category, is better than me."

"Nullifying the value?"

"Pretty much."

"In a sense," he said, "you're right: Your leadership flies off in opposite directions."

She wore an I-told-you-so-expression.

He continued, "That hypothetical woman who pulls in her horns—Remember her? You told me, no, you're not like that. But think again."

"Well," she said, "truth be told, relationships have never been my strong suit. They've always lost out to getting things done and getting ahead. There was a lot of schmoozing on our block in North Chicago, barbecues and what not, and"—she curled her lip—"I hardly showed my face."

She'd written off relationships, he noted, taken a defeatist attitude toward that side of life. "But you are in good shape with your team."

"Can't do it by myself. But that's just with people located here. Anyone remote, I don't keep up with. Not that I feel good about that."

"Is there something that warns you off of relationships?"

"Sanford, what am I going to do with you?" But she yielded to his influence. "You want to know the truth? I worry, to this day, whether people like me. A grown woman—can you believe it?!"

"I can. Social anxiety; it's as common as weeds."

"Plain language?" she asked.

"You're afraid of being rejected."

"Afraid of it? I am a reject," she said mournfully.

"*Re-ject*—thrown back." He couldn't restrain his literalist self.

"In middle school, the better-off girls had nicer clothes than I did. They wore a different blouse every day. I wore the same one. They'd corner me. 'You're a nobody,' they'd shriek. In eighth grade, I got into a screaming match with one of them, possibly the most sadistic of the bunch. The assistant principal came along just as it was about to turn violent. Guess what: After that, those kids more or less left me alone."

Quite the warrior, he said to himself. They refreshed their drinks.

"You say my leadership flies off in the opposite direction?" she started again.

"Yes. Is it possible to drive too hard for results?" asked Sanford.

"Nope. The more, the better. Did I tell you I run marathons?"

She hadn't.

"Well, on race day, if I fail to break four hours, it's a complete letdown," she said.

Sanford wasn't surprised. Her athletic figure bordered on the intimidating, and her competitive nature was always center stage.

"It's not okay if you miss by just a few seconds?" he asked, probing the depths of her competitive nature.

"Doesn't matter. Disappointment hangs over me for months."

"All or nothing?" he asked.

"Definitely," she said. "Oh, I haven't told you: My manager did the second part of my appraisal. 'You need to be more of an enterprise leader,' he told me. 'You're too focused on your own patch.'"

"Interesting. What's the message, really?"

She squinted. "I'm trying too hard?"

With his hand, he motioned for more.

She squinted again. "I'm overcompensating?"

Sanford nodded and smiled.

She sighed. "Do you mind if I have dinner by myself? Can that be arranged? Sorry, I know it's rude."

There was ground he planned to cover, but he went along. "Under one condition: that you don't work over dinner."

"Deal."

Walking back to her room, she thought, *He's growing on me.* But her mind was still a great jumble. Unable to sleep, she tried out the shower, which sported seventeen shower heads. Sanford had arranged for her to have that room, one of the nicer suites of the hotel.

She turned the shower handle, gingerly at first. Nozzles ringed the shower enclosure, some at chest level, some higher, some lower. It's nice, she thought; let's see what it can do. She turned the spray way up, then the heat. Now the water came coursing out, completely surrounding her, and it was getting hotter. The spray turned into needles on her skin, hitting sensitive parts of her body, and the heat was getting to be too much.

Typical, she thought. *You overshot.* She reached for the handles, but the shower stall had turned into a steam room, as thick with vapor as heavy fog. Now she was overwhelmed. It was like being overtaken by a higher power, and it wasn't benign. Bad associations crowded in, vague at first. She leaned back against the wall, but nozzles poked her. Her legs gave way, and she slid to a crouch.

In seconds, she was crying. It was nothing she'd experienced since childhood, and her usual instinct to clamp down didn't kick in. "Unwanted" flashed through her mind, slamming into her like a punch to the solar plexus; she sobbed all the harder. "Never amount to anything" quickly followed and dealt her another body blow. Then "Not college material" hit her, and her whole body jerked. Great waves of feeling bent her over, and she convulsed with sobs. The shower stall had gotten so steamed up that it was hard to breathe. She slipped to the tile floor, sobbing and gasping. As she sat there like a helpless child, the water pelted her from above.

Shielding the top of her head with her hands, she watched the water circle, around and around, swirling and swirling, sluicing down the drain. *Drained*, she thought.

Finally, she took a deep breath, put her hands on the floor of the shower, and mustered the strength to hoist herself up through the steamy air. She felt around with her hands, finally finding the handles one at a time and turning off the shower. Toweling off, she leaned against the wall to keep her knees from buckling.

Sanford was always interested in who showed up on the second morning. Right away, he could tell something was different. Her face was puffy, her voice deeper, more resonant. She seemed much more present, as if her armor, her self-protective gear, was gone.

"Pray tell," he said, sympathy in his voice.

"Last night was so big I almost can't see past it."

"Then don't," he said brightly. He handed her a leather-bound journal. "Here, write it all down."

"But this is yours. You've written on it."

He took it back, ripped out the only page he had written on, and handed it to her.

"But it's yours," she protested, this time without conviction.

He waved that off.

Warmed by his gesture, she bent to the task. A few minutes later, she looked up. "Rather than making you read this, I'll just tell you." She took a deep breath. "I don't know what hit me. That room you put me in, all those shower heads, water spurting at me from all directions, the heat, the fogged-up stall. I started sobbing and couldn't stop. What really got to me: memories, bad ones. They bent me over, shaking me like a spastic. Somehow, it was satisfying, though, like a bottle of champagne shaken and then uncorked. Like being purged."

"Released?"

"Yes, I've been released—from bondage. From bondage. Freed up from my single-minded campaign to . . ."

He waited.

"To prove my worth."

EmmaJean continued, "You see, I was an unwanted child. I overheard my mother say it, that I was a 'mistake.' It fit. I'm ten years younger than my middle sister." Her eyes glistened. "That's not all. My father put me down, and his harsh words still ring in my ears. 'You'll never amount to anything.' He flung it in my face like a stinking rag." Now she was angry. "I can remember walking back to my room on the unpainted plywood floor muttering, 'You bastard, I'll show you.'"

Sanford spoke up gently. "Let's go back to where we started, can we? Who are you?"

For the first time, she understood the question. "I'm not nothing. I'm not. I'm not!"

Sanford squeezed her hand. "You've fought really hard for that, haven't you?

"I have! I've been on a crusade."

"To negate the negation?"

"Exactly!" she said. In her mind, she had pronounced herself guilty any time she fell short, guilty as charged by her father—of worthlessness. Despite her soaring career and the considerable talents and abundant energy that drove it, self-doubt hung around her like a summer heatwave in a big city, moist, heavy, and foul.

"Another thing I'm not: I'm not that little girl anymore, that poor cursed suffering little girl. The curse is lifting.

"Who am I? I'm a devoted mother, a doting mother. Uh, maybe a bit too doting—whatever that's about. I'm a loyal wife whose love for her husband has been stopped up. Because . . ."

He waited.

"Because there was something wrong with me, and I didn't want him to see it." Tears rolled down her cheeks.

Ashamed, he thought, but it didn't need saying.

"No excuses, but my father had a hard life. I'd like to think he had it on the tip of his tongue to say, 'I didn't mean it, EmmaJean; don't take those hurtful words to heart.'" Now her eyes were wet again.

He recalled a passing thought he'd had early on, when EmmaJean was so reluctant. That if she could ever come to trust him, it might carry over.

This is a cautionary tale about a high-potential senior leader who had trouble accepting feedback.

NOTHING BUT THE BEST

P hilip Konig had been recruited personally by the megabank's CEO, Martin Middleton. His mandate: to fix investment banking. But much more that, Philip was brought in to be the heir apparent to replace Middleton. There were rumblings about Philip, to which Middleton turned a deaf ear, but the corporate head of HR, Frank Brescia, did not.

Let the Game Begin

Frank personally tried to help Philip but didn't get very far. So he decided to call in reinforcements—a leadership consultant—and set up a meeting with him to break the news. In dark suits, white shirts, and ties, they both arrived on time and went straight to the credenza and helped themselves to piping hot coffee. The striking high-floor view of the midtown cityscape didn't merit a glance.

Making the first move, Frank told Philip it was his turn to work with a leadership specialist. "You're not being singled out. We're making this available to a number of senior people."

Never mind that Philip was the first. "Can I get back to you by the end of the week?" Philip said. He wanted time to find out directly from the CEO what this was all about.

Later in the day, Philip caught up with Martin as he was packing up his briefcase. Philip knocked a couple of times on the open door.

"Come in, Philip," Martin said, giving him his full attention. "What's up?"

"Frank wants me to work with a shrink. Am I in trouble?"

"You should know better than that," Martin replied.

Philip was reassured but thought better of asking whether it was voluntary.

"I know the guy," Martin said. "His name is Jake, and he's good at this. If I had more runway, I'd do this myself."

Like a throwaway, he added: "He went to fancy schools, if that matters."

"Okay, boss, sign me up," Philip said, sounding like he meant it. He always wanted to be in his superior's good graces.

To his surprise, Philip took to the leadership consultant right away and wasted no time in telling his wife, Camille, about him. They were sitting in their spanking-new kitchen.

"His name is Jake Waverly. Martin thinks highly of him. I'd like him to meet you and the kids." Actually, Philip wanted to show her off; Camille had been quite the catch. The kids were appealing too, cute and smart. As was their big house, with its beautifully landscaped yard.

"Hold your horses," she said, palms out. Camille's pleasant expression wasn't skin-deep, but she had her limits.

"What horses? You're the one who rides." Actually, Philip admired her daring in riding horses and the figure she cut: jodhpurs, riding boots, blazer, and helmet. But his joke fell flat, and he pressed on. "Look, this isn't just about work; it's also about what I'm like outside of work. The real endgame here is to replace Martin one day."

"Then, sure. Why not?" she said, good sport that she was.

He kissed her hand in thanks. He had an idea that he wasn't the easiest guy in the world to live with. He was lucky in love, and he knew it.

The next time Jake was in town, they had him over to the house. As Philip showed him around, Jake said all the right things. Over dinner, Jake proved able to engage the kids in conversation, always a trick. Once they peeled off, he and Camille talked at length about the helping professions and various "treatment modalities," as she termed them. She had a social work degree. Seeing them connect, Philip said to himself, *Chalk it up!*

"I hope it wasn't an imposition, having me over," Jake said to Camille.

"Not at all," she replied, and Philip didn't think she was pretending.

Jake had planned to take a limo back to the hotel, but over his objections, Philip drove him there. He had the top down on his antique Jaguar. Wind noise kept conversation to a minimum.

The Middle Game

Once Jake finished interviewing Philip's coworkers and the report was ready, they met upstate at a luxurious faux-French chateau.

Built in the 1920s as a private residence, it boasted turrets, lead-ed-pane casement windows, a slate roof, and an indoor swimming pool with Italian tiles and floor-to-ceiling windows. It was the sort of thing that would impress Philip.

They met in the boardroom with a long mahogany table. Philip was nattily turned out—worsted gray slacks, a blue dress shirt, and a blazer with a neatly folded white handkerchief tucked in its breast pocket. An expensive-looking watch sat prominently on his left wrist. He could have passed as lord of the manor. The fine figure he cut was only marred by a bit of bulge at the waistline.

Jake motioned to Philip to take the chair at the head of the table, and he opened enthusiastically: "The good news is very good indeed!" This brought a broad smile to Philip's face. "People sing your praises like it's the 'Hallelujah Chorus': 'Gloria in excelsis deo!'"

Philip didn't object to the hyperbole.

"One thing's for sure," Jake went on, "you've worked wonders with investment banking."

"Right. I'm amazed by how well you can get an organization to perform. It just exceeds your wildest expectations," exclaimed Philip. The thrill of high achievement rippled through his body. When Philip had taken over, only fixed income and institutional bonds were performing. Everything else was lackluster at best— M&A, trading, and equities.

Jake noticed the sun was in Philip's eyes and lowered the blinds. "One of your peers told me you want to make it the top firm of its kind anywhere," said Jake.

"It's true!" Philip said. "I've been on a crusade to do just that. You get it rolling, and you move heaven and Earth to make it happen.

You've done it so many times it isn't an accident. But you've got to put it together right—that's key—and that means recruiting the best and the brightest. I scour the world, literally. God, we have one of the best staffs in the world. If you've gone to one of the top schools, that really puts the thumbprint on you."

"Martin agrees. Quote, 'Philip has almost an uncanny ability to find the highest-performing people in a discipline.' Credit to you, Philip: Some people are too insecure to hire the best. Oh, and you're a talent junkie, someone said."

"Can't be too addicted to talent."

"Let's not forget: You look after that talent, you refurbish their offices to a high standard, and you let them do their jobs."

"Not doing that is like buying a Porsche 911 when you can't afford to park in an expensive garage."

Jake sent him off to "bask in the glory," as he put it. The chateau's grounds were expansive and nicely landscaped. Philip enjoyed the park but couldn't help comparing it unfavorably to Blenheim Palace, the steep drop-off to the pond. But there was no basking. That's not how his mind worked.

He returned to find a magazine with his photo on the cover. It was the current issue of the industry rag, *The Banker*. He looked every bit the master of the universe.

"Impressive," Jake said.

That was what Philip craved, precisely that word of all words he most wanted to hear—although he had never spelled it out in his mind. "I was thrilled when it came out," he said. "Lots of congratulations. I gulped all that down, but it wasn't long before I was thirsty for more—parched even."

"People say nice things about this?" Jake asked.

"Pretty much, yes. Felt good."

"How about Martin?"

"Nothing. Not a peep."

"Maybe he didn't see it."

"Oh, he saw it. I put a copy on his desk."

"How much does that matter?"

"More than I care to admit." Philip looked Jake over. "You see, I was the firstborn on both sides of the family. 'Our hopes are resting on you,' they said. I did my best, that's for sure. But I've got this superhuman image that's impossible to live up to."

Just as Jake was about to speak, Philip added, "There's more. You know how people will say he's always there for his kids. My father wasn't. I was a star pitcher in high school. My senior year, I even got scouted by the major leagues. My father didn't come to a single game. My mother would tell me, 'Your father is very proud of you.' But that didn't count."

"It left a hole?"

"Which can't be filled," replied Philip.

They broke for lunch but first Philip returned phone calls. All in all, Jake was pleased with how the morning went. Philip was into it, and that meant a lot to Jake, a relationship guy. The connection they'd made, he believed, would carry them through the rough stuff ahead.

Lunch was served in the same room, a tablecloth laid at the other end of the table. The meal dulled Jake's senses. He poured himself coffee from a fresh pot and said, "Take a few minutes to make an entry in your journal: What has struck you so far? Let me know when you're done. I'll be sitting over there." He pointed to a spare chair pushed against the wall.

He tried to quiet his mind, which he could usually do no matter what was going on. But something was bothering him. Ah, Philip overrated himself; that was it. Typically, that meant the person was defensive and had trouble with criticism. But it could also mean achieving is all-important. Jake recalled asking Martin if they'd leveled with Philip. The answer was, "We tried."

Jake was startled back to reality by Philip's voice, which sounded different. "Can we get on with it—please?" That tacked-on *please* didn't help.

"Sure. But let's bridge into it. Is there anything missing from the set of good things about you?"

"You first." Clearly, he was in no mood for games.

"Okay," Jake said. Normally, Jake would have tried one more time, but there was no room to maneuver. "Recapping: Kudos for turning around investment banking and for recruiting great people to do that. What's missing is how you work with people."

Philip sneered. "That's what you're going on?! What's not there?"

Jake's stomach hurt. "No, of course not," he said in a level tone. "This is based on the interviews, on people's ratings."

"Which people? Just come out with it, will you please?"

Philip's tone grated on Jake, but he was not about to fight fire with fire. Nor was he about to proceed as planned—to unspool people's comments and let Philip draw his own conclusions. He junked that plan on the spot. That would never work. Instead, Jake decided he'd feed Philip the summary points, the headlines, one at a time. "Mainly," he started, "your people, your direct reports—"

"Ingrates. Where would they be without me?"

Who needs this? Jake thought, understanding why management hadn't been straight with Philip.

"On the contrary, they are grateful for the opportunity, every single one of them. Of course they are. That came through loud and clear."

"At least on that their heads are screwed on straight." Philip eased up a little.

"Right. But I'd be less than honest if I didn't say they're frustrated," Jake said and recoiled inside: *"Less than honest": I never use that phrase.*

"What do you mean frustrated!? Be specific."

Again, Philip was on the offensive, hammering away. If Jake were treated this way in his private life, he wouldn't put up with it. But here, he felt he had no choice but to master his feelings. "You don't involve them enough, seek their counsel. You think you do, but you don't."

"Bull crap!" shouted Philip.

Jake, like the conductor of an orchestra, made a *pianissimo* gesture, to take it down several notches.

Philip lowered his voice but continued in the same vein. "My staff has lots of influence. Their expectations are too high."

Jake wasn't sure where to go next. Then he had an idea. "You're right: Expectations are often the culprit. Do you know what the Buddhists say?"

"No, tell me." For the moment, he seemed mollified or distracted.

"Expectations are the root of all suffering."

"*Their* expectations, that is." Philip paused. "Maybe mine too." He calmed down as abruptly as he got riled up.

Jake's stomach stopped hurting. *There's still hope*, he thought.

"Let's take a look at the numbers, shall we?" Philip didn't object. "See," he said, pointing to a table, "you were rated down on listening, and you were rated down on being open to pushback."

"I reject the data," Philip said.

Jake almost fell out of his chair. "Hey, you're an analytical guy. How is it you have no use for this data?"

"This is soft stuff. I'm a hard-numbers guy."

I'm running out of options, Jake thought and began to despair. But he came up with another move. "You know that hard numbers aren't always as hard as rock, right?"

Philip listened.

"Neither are so-called soft numbers always as squishy as marshmallows. Anyway, let's take a peek at the personality profile, which I happen to know is sound psychometrically. Remember: You're the only one who filled it out."

"Okay. But spare me the detail."

He was behaving better, so Jake gave him the upshot: that Philip is hard to influence. "Sir, does the tool fit the pattern or not?" Jake asked. "Will you grace the viewing audience with your answer?"

"Fits."

"Right. Give the man a prize." That comment was an attempt to be playful that didn't backfire. But he had no illusions he'd changed Philip's mind.

"I'm still not buying it. Things have settled down since that survey was administered. We'll have to redo it."

"Anytime you want," Jake said, without for a minute believing the findings would be different. He tried a different tack. "In the meantime, can we agree to disagree?" He knew it was useless to press his case.

But Philip got hot again. "I have a problem with this conversation. It's way out of context. The CEO is unbelievably autocratic; this picture of me pales by comparison."

It wasn't lost on Jake that Philip had indirectly admitted to the criticism. "Are you a fan of constructive tension?" he asked. "Intellectually speaking."

"Yeah, nothing like a good debate."

"Then can we agree to disagree?" asked Jake.

Philip nodded.

"A bitter pill, I know. I wish it were otherwise."

"It's not your fault," Philip said.

The Endgame Begins

They parted amicably, to Jake's immense relief. It wasn't until he closed the door to his room—he had arranged to stay over—that he realized how worn down he was. Like wearing leather shoes to go scrambling on granite boulders. He changed clothes, took a run, and had dinner in his room. Feeling like himself again, he sat down in an upholstered chair and put his feet up on the hassock. In a forgiving mood, he thought, *It's not Philip's fault,* the *way he reacted today. He could thank his parents and grandparents for that.* Jake was not about to give up on Philip. He knew that the least likely prospects can surprise you, just as the most promising prospects can fizzle out.

Jake's mind jumped to something he had been told in the strictest confidence by the head of trading, Sheila Armistead. Philip had met her at a conference, stayed in touch, and recruited her heavily for this position. She'd known that Philip had worked his way up in trading, had been a stellar performer in his day. But she hadn't been prepared for this: He dropped by the trading floor practically every day and chatted people up, glancing at their blinking screens that kept refreshing. She'd only been onboard for nine months and felt strongly that his visits undermined her, given that she was new, an underling, and—to boot—a woman.

It took her weeks to work up the nerve to say something to Philip. One day, walking by his office, she saw the door was open and knocked. He motioned her in. As she began to speak, she saw he was looking at the computer screen. He was still doing emails. Finally, he turned her way, and she felt her face flush. But she blurted it out. "Philip, I'm trying to establish myself, and your presence on the floor doesn't help. It gives people the impression you don't trust me."

"No, I don't think so. Wouldn't they think it strange, given my background, if I didn't walk the floor? I think they like my little visits."

"Sure, up to a point. But don't you see you're overindexing?"

"Frankly, I don't."

"You have them looking to you, not me," said Sheila.

"Hey, you're doing great. Don't worry about it."

Meanwhile, Back at Home

Philip was able to get home from the feedback meeting in time for dinner. In the car, he had put himself on notice: You're not going to walk in there and unload on them. It took him the whole drive back to turn the mental heat down to simmer. Fake it 'til you make it, he instructed himself.

Camille had prepared one of his favorite meals, slow-cooked brisket, potatoes, and carrots, along with a green salad. Everyone took their usual spots at the kitchen table. He asked the kids about their days but studiously avoided saying anything about his. Afterward, he washed the dishes. He always did, preferring to do it by hand. He knew it wasn't much, but, in his mind, something was better than nothing. He didn't want a repeat of the time when Camille lost all patience with him: "You don't lift a finger around here." It wasn't only that; he wanted to be good. He wanted to be better than his father.

He thought he'd done a decent acting job, but when he spotted Camille standing in the doorway, waiting quietly for him to finish up, he could tell otherwise. She took his hand and, without a word, led him from the kitchen to the sunroom. It had glass walls on three sides—a "wing of light," the architect had called it. It gave out onto the lush, closely cropped lawn with woods behind it. He called it the conservatory. She closed the door behind her. Gently, she said, "So, Philip, how did it go?" She sat down on the settee, but he took a chair.

He surprised himself by coming right out with it. "Terrible. Those ingrates, they slammed me." But he had no desire to get specific with her. That would be like walking around the house with no shirt on, putting on display his unsightly midriff.

She asked him to elaborate.

"Another time," he said.

"Whatever it is, I know you're not perfect, but I expected better than this—from those people. Cripes!"

Her loyalty loosened him up, and he reversed roles. "Could there be a kernel of truth to it?—could be," he said. "But I have to admit, Camille, there was good stuff too. Very good stuff, actually." Some of the gratified feeling paid him a return visit.

"Well deserved, I'm sure about that," Camille said. Having her on his side meant a lot to him. "But it must hurt a lot after all you've done for those people," she said.

Philip choked up. Camille went over to him and motioned to him to stand up. Reluctant at first, he got up and buried his face in the crook of her neck. Only with Camille did he feel safe enough to show his emotions.

As they sat down again, now next to each other on the settee, she asked, "So what did they say?"

"What's the knock on me? Basically, I'm hardheaded." A little laugh escaped him.

"No big surprise, right?" she said, laughing along with him.

One of their kids called for her, and, with a squeeze on his arm, off she went. But that was okay. In just a few minutes, she had done him a world of good. She was the person in his life best able to influence him. That is, if she put her foot down.

The previous spring, he'd gotten it into his head to buy a forty-eight-foot sailboat with berths for the whole family—a Hinckley, naturally. He salivated over that boat like it was a sirloin hamburger or a Häagen-Dazs ice cream cone. Excited, he'd shown her striking photos of the boat. The expression on her face told him she didn't share his enthusiasm. He backed off. He wanted the boat, but he also wanted to stay in her good graces. It was a lot of money, and how much would they use it anyway? Over some Lavazza espresso the next morning, he was gracious in defeat. "Not every idea is a good idea," he said. Actually, that was her line.

They had recently moved into their house, custom built. The great room with its soaring ceiling featured a fieldstone fireplace. The stonework was meant to duplicate a retaining wall that had appeared in *Architectural Digest*. A photo of it was pinned to the contractor's bulletin board. Philip had returned from a trip to Asia to visit investment banking's outposts there—Hong Kong, Shanghai, Tokyo—to find the fireplace almost finished. At first blush, he was pleased—a fieldstone fireplace, how about that?

But a moment later, he realized it wasn't what he wanted, wasn't what was spec'd. This one didn't have a mantel; the concrete between the stones was exposed. The intended version was meant to use ashlar masonry, where the stones are cut and arrayed so that the upper ones appear to be supported by the lower ones; the concrete is hidden.

He called the contractor. There had been a mix-up. The mason they'd wanted wasn't available. He called Camille, who had seen the fireplace the day before. "It's got to come down," he said.

"Do you have to?"

Rhetorical question. He did have to. He had the contractor rebuild the fireplace, with a mantel this time and better-looking fieldstones. People would later call it a work of art, which always gave Philip a little shot of pleasure.

The Saturday following Philip's tumultuous insight meeting, he and Camille went for a walk. It had rained for days, and they took advantage of a break in the weather, although the sky was still gray. Holding hands, they chatted about this and that. After a while, she turned to him. "So, Philip, can we talk about the input you got this week? Can you stand to?" She looked into his eyes, appealing to him.

He wanted to be responsive to her, and yet he had no stomach for the subject. "This is so pleasant," Philip said. "Can't we keep it that way?"

"Believe me, I'd prefer that too."

They walked on in silence, still holding hands. He wanted to shut down any further conversation on that sore subject, but he knew she meant well. If there were one person whose loyalty he could count on, it was her. As they rounded the big loop, he forced these words out of his mouth: "Okay, we can talk about it."

She squeezed his hand. Treading gingerly, she asked, "Has it been on your mind?"

He nodded and grimaced.

"Painful subject, I know," she said.

It was his turn to squeeze her hand. Gestures were all he could produce. It began to drizzle but soon stopped.

"You've been a huge success," she said. She looked at him, and he met her gaze. "But this is a chance to be better."

He didn't say anything, just started walking again, without reaching for her hand.

She caught up with him, saying, "Here's a thought. Can I offer it?"

He made himself say yes.

"Talk with Elena. You trust her, right?" Elena, his whiz kid CFO who more than held her own with her older colleagues, was the one person on his staff he was truly at ease with. A lot of that was her. She was outgoing, genuine, comfortable with herself. She was close to their family, came over for dinner from time to time. Unattached at the time, she once even volunteered to take care of the kids for the weekend so that Philip and Camille could get away.

"Okay, I'll do it," he said.

The next morning, Sunday, he came bouncing into the kitchen and gave Camille a big hug. "I've got an idea." They took their coffee to the conservatory; the kids weren't up yet. "We've got more money than we know what to do with, even with my extravagant tastes. Let's step up our giving." He believed strongly that when much is given, much is expected.

"Nice, Philip." She patted his hand. "Big Brothers Big Sisters, that's what I suggest. They do a lot of good for kids in need. You could join the board, made up of types like you."

"Spare me the board seat. I've got no patience for that, a bunch of guys pontificating," he said. "Okay, Big Brothers Big Sisters. What else?"

"There are plenty of worthy agencies out there," Camille said.

"Nah, let's create our own agency—more control—and you run it," he said. "With the kids growing up, you've been casting around for ways to fill the void. Am I right?"

"I like that idea," she said, eyes bright.

"Good, it's settled."

"Just a sec. Where are you in this setup?" she asked.

"I'd help."

"What if I don't want your help?" she asked with a smirk.

"How could you not?" he said, acting like he was offended. "My help—you can take it or leave it."

"Put it in the bylaws, just to make sure," she said.

"You can't be serious." But he had documents drawn up that demarcated their respective roles. Camille pronounced herself satisfied, giving him reason to feel good about himself.

Adding Elena to the Mix

Jake was surprised when Philip's assistant called to set up a meeting with not just Philip but Elena too. With Philip's okay, Jake called Elena before the three of them met. "This is very awkward for me," she said. "I can't speak for everyone."

Jake reassured her. "Right. Just speak for yourself."

They met in the same conference room where Philip heard he needed help. Jake went over to the window. "Fabulous view," he said.

Philip turned to Jake for an opening comment.

"It's your show," Jake said.

"Yeah, it was Camille's idea," said Philip, and then turned to Elena. "People on the team say I'm hard to influence. What do you think? Is it true?" He looked expectantly at her.

"I can't speak for everyone," Elena said. "But based on what I've observed, there's some truth to that, yes."

"They're not piling on?" asked Philip.

"I haven't seen their comments, of course, but, no, I don't think so," replied Elena.

Philip was silent, glum.

Jake spoke. "You've brought in great people, right? By definition, they have a lot to offer. That's the whole idea, right?"

"Right, that's the whole idea. They're very, very good at what they do," said Philip. "I wouldn't settle for less."

"What do you think those star-quality people want?" asked Jake.

"Let Elena say," said Philip.

She leaned forward. "They're dying to contribute, to do a good job in their area, naturally."

"Don't I let them do that?!"

"You do, certainly in my case, and I don't think I'm alone."

"Isn't that enough!?" Philip shot back.

"Can I refresh your drinks?" Jake asked. Elena handed him her half-empty glass. Philip helped himself to more coffee.

"Another question," Jake said. "What else do talented people, highly motivated people, want?"

Philip had a ready answer. "To have challenging jobs, to get recognized for their good work, to be rewarded financially."

"Yes. Anything else?" Jake said.

"Hell if I know," said Philip.

"Elena?" Jake asked, turning to her.

She shot him a *Thanks a lot!* glance.

"Have you two planned this whole thing out?" Philip said.

"Are you kidding?" she said, clearly insulted.

Philip held up both hands, conceding defeat.

"What else could people possibly want?" she said. "To chip in their two cents' worth sometimes."

"I hadn't thought of that," said Philip.

Look, he can listen! Jake said to himself.

The following week, Jake and Philip held their planning meeting in the same room.

"That Elena is something else," Philip said brightly.

"Yes, she was a big help," Jake said.

"Remind me," Philip said, "what's the purpose of this meeting?"

"You know, to get specific about the changes you'll make."

Philip gave him a blank look.

"Are you up for this?" Jake asked.

"Not really," said Philip.

"But I thought—"

"Think what you want," Philp said, none too friendly.

"Does that mean you've decided not to change?"

"Why mess with a winning formula?" said Philip.

"Would you mind writing that down?" said Jake, holding out a pad and pen.

Ignoring the offer, Philip said, "I haven't decided not to change, but I am sure I've given you that impression."

Amused by Philip's cleverness, Jake still felt duty bound to keep at it: "Those were your people speaking. To do nothing is to thumb your nose at them. For your own self-preservation, you'd better do something."

"I take your point. It's appreciated," said Philip.

"Shall we get down to brass tacks?" asked Jake.

"Not today."

He's got me coming and going, Jake thought and decided to come at it from a different angle. "Philip, could fear be operating?"

"I suppose so."

"Where is it, then, the fear?"

"Behind me," Philip said.

"Take a look?"

"Can't," replied Philip.

There you have it, Jake thought. "I have a hunch. About what the fear is about," he said aloud. "Do you want to hear it?"

"Some other time." Philip's voice was small and real as rain.

"You sidled up to it; that's good for now." Jake was not about to push through Philip's defenses. They were there for a reason.

And So the Game Ends

A month later, Philip acted like he hadn't learned a thing. The CEO had charged him, along with his peers, with rolling out a diversity and inclusion initiative. Since this was Martin's personal initiative, Philip went all out. Aggressive hiring targets. Two days of diversity-and-inclusiveness training for all IB managers. An evaluation of the senior team's inclusive leadership, followed by a day of data-driven team building. And, separately, a two-hour feedback meeting for each team member. This was the plan.

When he unveiled it to his staff, he was greeted by stunned silence. His most senior person, Kevin, was the first to speak.

"Look, Philip, we're all for this; we'll grab talent wherever we can find it." Nods all around. "But you've gone overboard." Nods to that too, and murmurs.

Someone else chimed in, none too friendly: "You've got to scale this back, Philip; you've got to." A kind of emotional contagion set in.

"Now, wait a minute," Philip insisted. "This is important."

"No question about that," said Kevin. "But, like I said, you've gone overboard"—and as if warming to his metaphor—"and sunk to the ocean floor."

Chuckles all around. Philip's face turned red. He looked at Elena for support.

She just shrugged her shoulders but, a moment later, spoke up: "Okay," she said to her peers, "if this is too ambitious, why don't we all get specific on how to scale it back."

A chorus of support for that idea broke out.

But Philip was having none of it. In a fit of pique, he said, "I'm getting nowhere," and left the room.

What his team couldn't know is that he came honestly by his stance toward higher-ups. Nor did they care. They already knew full well Philip was all too good at managing up.

"Growing up," Philip had told Jake, "I could never understand why other kids didn't do what their parents or teachers told them to do. Thankfully, my kids are the same way. My oldest just told me, 'I want to please you and Mom; your opinion means so much to me.'"

When Jake heard about the meeting, his hopes for Philip came crashing down like a child falling from a high branch.

Six months later, Philip was terminated. To the very end, Martin, the CEO, was reluctant to part with him. It wasn't just IB's lush profits. He never stopped believing in Philip, wanted to give him more time to come around with Jake's help. But his hand was forced, and his own credibility was at stake.

In his handling of Philip's exit, though, he was most considerate. There was no way that Philip would be ushered unceremoniously, ignominiously, out of the building, a not-uncommon if brutal practice in corporations. He was given ten weeks to find another job and allowed to keep his office. But that special treatment did Philip no favors.

Elena called Jake to let him know in case he hadn't heard. He hadn't. His first thought was, *Oh no, the disgrace.* Philip's worst fear.

Elena had seen it coming, but she was still very upset—for Philip, for the family, and, frankly, for herself. Unlike her colleagues, she had seen another side to Philip: open to influence—hers, at least—and even childlike in seeking her counsel.

Jake wrote Philip to say how sorry he was. "Let me know when you're ready to talk."

In the meantime, Philip continued to go into the office, to take his lunch in the executive dining room. He was determined to hold his head high. But his staff hardly acknowledged him, like he had turned into a leper. No one but Elena sat with him at lunch, and not every day. She knew it was not a good idea to associate herself too closely with him.

In the fourth week, he received a job offer, a good one, and he accepted. The offer was no surprise; he remained highly marketable. That Friday, his last day in the office, he and Elena had lunch. "It's been ghastly," Elena said, "like somebody died."

Twisting his mouth oddly, he said, "Murdered, more like."

She couldn't help it: *Suicide* leapt to mind, and at that, she felt disloyal, all the more so for beginning to think of herself, *How much more of this can I take?*

"I take that back," he said. "Truth is, it was a self-inflicted wound."

The following week, Philip called Jake. He was chipper. "I landed a plum job at a big London-based bank. It means a move, but Camille and I are satisfied that it comes at a good time in our kids' lives."

"Congratulations. But I'm sorry it came to this. I wish I could have done more."

"You did what you could," said Philip. "You put the ugly truth in front of me. I couldn't handle it."

"I give you a lot of credit for coming to see it that way."

"Late in the game. Oh, well."

Jake decided to call the question. "Philip, do you think I spilled the beans?"

"For a moment, that possibility went through my mind. But, no, they knew all along. That's why they brought in someone like you."

"That's a relief. Another thing: In your new job, you'll have a clean slate." It seemed that Jake couldn't stop wanting him to change.

"Yeah, we'll see if I've learned anything," said Philip.

"I have faith in you."

Silence. "I asked Elena to come with me. She turned me down," Philip said, his voice cracking.

"That must really hurt."

Philip nodded, emotion all over his face.

"They say there's no knowledge without suffering. Do you believe that?"

Philip took a deep breath. "Yes, I do."

PROLOGUE

Veri Archer, an operating executive in her midforties, is recruited to be CEO of a high-tech start-up, replacing the founder-CEO, Sanjay Cherry. He stays on as CTO. For Veri, it becomes a rite of passage twice over.

SUCCEEDING SANJAY

Veri Archer decided to get some stress out of her system. What better way than an 8:00 p.m. run on the track of the local high school in Belmont, a town just outside of Boston? She'd taken up running in her thirties.

"Isn't it late to be doing this?" her husband, Lance, a detective in the Cambridge Police Department, said.

"It's okay," she said. "The track is lit."

He just shrugged his shoulders.

As she walked from the parking lot to the track, she was startled to be approached by a teenaged girl.

"Sorry to bother you, but I'm trying to raise money for the girls Ultimate Frisbee club."

"You remind me of me," said Veri. "How much do you need to meet your goal?"

"Well, $250," the teenager replied.

"I don't have any money with me, but call me tomorrow at MobileAdTech, where I work, and I'll donate $500."

Veri didn't mention she was CEO. She was much too humble to do that. She had earned a degree in computer science from MIT and went to work for Cisco. In her last job, she ran a division much larger than MobileAdTech.

She had fashioned herself into quite the operational leader. She often said, "There's always a better way." It had been one of her father's dictums. And it played out at home too. Her husband, Lance, jokingly called her a "method-ist." She was a good sport about it, but the teasing did not diminish one whit her passion for making things better.

Her Rallying Cry

She had been approached by a recruiter for the MobileAdTech job. Neal Armbruster, the board's lead director, had explained to Veri, the top candidate, "Sanjay's no manager, and, really, he's got no desire to be. So he's happy—well, not entirely happy—to let some-one 'do all that day-to-day crap,' as he would put it." Neal said, "We need someone to get this house in order, someone just like you." The company had grown to the point that it needed professional management.

To Veri, that didn't just mean operational effectiveness; it also meant getting costs under control. Ultimately, it meant getting the company into the black. "Stop the bleeding" was her reason for being. It was like the finish line for the 5K and 10K races she ran. But she didn't tell Neal or anyone in the company. It was her silent rallying cry.

A Delicate Situation

Against the odds and despite the naysayers, Sanjay Cherry had, by native ability and force of will, brought his business dream to life. He'd invented a technology that enabled companies to advertise on mobile devices. Not only had he attracted paying customers, but he'd also raised millions of investor dollars. That was a while ago, but what matters is what happened later. As it turned out, he wasn't the man for the top job. The board felt the mismatch keenly. In their minds, the best remedy was a new CEO, and the board started the search without telling Sanjay.

Neal's venture fund had put up the seed money for the company and, later, was the biggest investor in the series A round of funding. A generation older than Sanjay, Neal was something of a father figure for him. Not every financier gets involved personally with the top person in a portfolio company, but that came naturally to Neal. But in pressing the founder to step down, Neal knew he was going out on a limb, one that could easily be sawed off behind him.

Neal and Sanjay were out to eat at a Vietnamese place they frequented—a late dinner, as usual. Over appetizers and a beer, they first talked sports, then turned to the company issues of the moment. Then Neal judged the moment to be right to raise the touchy subject.

"What do you mean?!" Sanjay snorted. "It's my baby."

"Yeah, it's your baby, but you're taking lousy care of it. I've been telling you that all along."

"Yeah, but I never expected it to come to this." Sanjay was combative; he was stricken.

Softening, Neal said, "Sanjay, you want your baby to grow up and be big and strong, right?"

"Of course I do." Neal sat and waited. "But with me as CEO, it never will—is that what you want me to say?"

"What do you say?" Neal asked.

Their waiter came by, and they ordered another beer, Kirin. "But it will look terrible," Sanjay offered, as if searching for justification.

"Yeah, and how will it look if the company never fulfills its promise because you were too proud to give up a role you're not good at?"

Sanjay swallowed. It wasn't beer. He hadn't touched the fresh bottle. The main course arrived. Sanjay went quiet, and Neal left him alone. The check arrived. It wasn't that much, but they both reached for the little plastic tray, and neither one would let go. They laughed; Neal yielded. Out on the sidewalk, they wished each other a friendly good night.

The next morning, Neal took an early flight home. When the plane touched down, he called Sanjay.

The first words out of Sanjay's mouth were, "Okay, okay, I'll do it."

When Neal told him about Veri, Sanjay said, "From a big corporation? You've got to be kidding."

Sanjay agreed to stay on, as CTO, reporting to Veri. No one really counted the cost of that arrangement, awkward at best.

Enter The Guide; That's Me

Neal brought me in as an insurance policy a few months after Veri started. "Sanjay's the brains of the operation, obviously," Neal told me. "But managerially, his legs are spindly, and those spindly legs will never carry the company where it needs to go. That's where someone like Veri comes in. Mind you, he's a good person; his ethics are pristine." Then Neal threw in "Sanjay likes food. I tell him, 'Get exercise.' He's never developed a taste for it, he said. Ha-ha."

On my first visit, Neal introduced me to Sanjay, a handsome guy sporting a black Ralph Lauren polo shirt. Not tall. Though cordial, he was less than enthusiastic.

Next, I was escorted to Veri's office. I was curious about her name. "It's a made-up name, derived from the Latin word for truth. My father's idea. He was forever saying, 'Always tell the truth.' I try to, to the best of my ability."

Her whitewashed office, no bigger than anyone else's, had none of the trappings of a CEO: gray Steelcase furniture; on her desk, a sixteen-ounce bottle of Diet Coke, half empty. Her crisp white shirt and pressed black slacks—never mind that jeans and T-shirts were de rigueur there—left no doubt that this was a professional woman meant to be taken seriously. Her thin nose looked like it was meant to cut through disorder. Her teeth were even and white as quartz.

She motioned to the small table and, with a flourish, plunked down a framed black-and-white photo. "You said you'd like to know something personal about me," she said, friendly as the rising sun. "Well, on a lark, I grabbed this as I was running out the door. If that child looks suspiciously like me, it's because it is." She took a sip of the soda.

I felt like saying that stuff, diet or not, isn't healthy. But she probably knew it anyway.

The young Veri is perched primly on an old-fashioned couch, her hands on her lap, demurely clasped. Her hair is fairly short, as was the custom at the time. She's smiling, dancing light in her side-turned eyes.

"After church, we'd go over to my grandparents' for lunch and pinochle. I was expected to be seen and not heard." She'd grown up Catholic in Iowa, went to parochial school throughout.

"Were you permitted to move?" Dumb question. I was still getting my footing. Thankfully, she didn't seem to notice.

"Of course," she said, laughing. "But I was just a kid, and I thought it best to stay put. I sat there reading books and listening in on the grown-ups' conversation." With a flourish, she brought out another photo.

Just then, there was a loud rapping on the door, which swung open. In walked Neal, radiating youthful energy, vibrant as a child racing around a playground. He shook my hand vigorously and kissed Veri lightly on both cheeks in the European manner.

"We're most fortunate to have Veri running the company," he said. "She's a great operating executive, the right person to shape up this company, to professionalize it."

Playing along, she got up and curtsied.

"But it's not like she has a free hand."

Veri's face clouded over for a moment, as if to say, *A free hand, ha!* But, aloud, she said, "Sanjay's great. Incredibly talented. And the fact is, without him, MobileAdTech would not exist." It sounded biblical, as if she attributed a godlike aspect to him. It turned out she wasn't the only one doing that.

Turning to me, Neal said, "I want Veri to have every advantage, and that's where you come in. It's no picnic working with a founder. Even good guys like Sanjay—it doesn't matter." He paused. "By the way, I'm not spared." He wished us well and took his leave.

"There's more to say—over lunch," said Veri. "In the meantime—" She brought out the second photo.

"Your life story told in pictures—what better way?"

"Why, thank you," Veri replied. All I saw was a black speck halfway up a rock face. "That's me, the first time I climbed, belayed of course. I took to it right away. My husband, who doesn't like heights, dubbed me 'the ebullient mountain goat.'"

"You're way up there!" It was abundantly clear that this was not a one-dimensional careerist.

Tough Cookie

Lunch from a Thai place was laid out on a long buffet table in the open area for everyone to enjoy. We helped ourselves and took the food back to her office.

"Hey, I've got an appointment coming up with the head of business development," she said. "Why don't you come along? Her name is Stephanie. I'll go make sure it's alright with her." She was back a minute later. "It's okay. By the way, she's one of seven direct reports—including Sanjay." She shot me a knowing smile.

The numbers for the quarter were on track. But there was one area where Stephanie had fallen short. Veri took her to task: "Remember: You're not a one-woman band."

"But it's quicker that way and easier," Stephanie objected. "Look at my results. Does it look like I need help?"

"C'mon, Stephanie. Where would you be if other people didn't open doors for you—Sanjay, especially, with all his connections. Remember: Leadership is a team sport. Otherwise, keep up the good work." That was that. No nonsense, efficient, on time.

"I can see you're one tough cookie when you need to be," I said, back in her office.

"Yeah, well, that's with someone on my staff. But Neal wants me to be more that way with Sanjay."

"Sanjay: That's a big topic. Shall we take a crack at it now?" I asked.

"Sure, what the heck? No time like the present."

"Okay, good. First of all, tell me what he's like."

"He's smart as a whip and technically versed like I've never seen, and I've worked with plenty of very sharp engineers. He never takes notes in meetings, remembers everything. He may actually be a genius.

"Personally," she continued, "he's friendly, polite, good manners. Opens the door for me, a real gentleman; chivalry isn't dead. I think he really cares about his people. But when he makes up his mind, it's like moving heaven and earth to sway him. He makes snap judgments about people, and it's like they're slotted forever. I've already resurrected a couple of good ones he gave up for dead."

"Are there things you need from him that you're not getting?" I asked.

"Yeah. To be open to systematizing things; he's not. And to stop launching R&D efforts unilaterally. He still acts like it's his prerogative."

"Not good."

"Look. He's got an iron will; how else would he have done what he's done here?"

Would she turn apologist, I asked myself, like so many people working with founders? Would she make excuses for him or stick to her guns?

She took a deep breath. "As for me—" She looked down, and for a few moments, her upper body shook. "Sorry, sorry," she said, her voice muffled with emotion. She got a tissue from her bag. "I never cry. Even with my family. Well, at a funeral maybe."

"Why now?" I had an idea but better that it come from her.

"He doesn't want me here." Her eyes brimmed with tears.

"Literally true or not, that's really hard to take."

She nodded, and the phone rang. She took a deep breath and said she had to take the call but arranged for us to meet again later that afternoon.

I expected we'd pick up where we'd left off, but no. She reached for another picture, this one of her as an adolescent.

"Oh," I said, "there you are in your Sunday best—white gloves, white dress, white veil, white patent-leather shoes."

"Not just any Sunday. It was my First Communion."

I felt stupid but plunged ahead. "Oh, was the church a big influence?"

"Yes and no. My parents weren't religious, but they believed the parochial schools were better. Just like the nuns, we had to wear a uniform. I took the theology literally for a long time. My parents didn't disabuse me."

"Were the nuns strict? That's what I hear."

"They didn't hesitate to discipline us, but they were not unkind, with just one exception. I've even stayed close to one of them, Sister Cristina. There was a discipline they imposed. You had to do things a certain way. They were very particular. You had to be detail oriented and organized. Little did they know they were preparing me to run ops!"

"Funny! Do you see a theme winding its way through all these telling bits and pieces?"

She danced away from my question, playfully. "Isn't that your job, to interpret?"

"True, but isn't it better if it comes from you?"

"Okay, if I must," she said, obligingly. "A good girl, a good Catholic girl. Obvious, isn't it?"

"Yes. Can you take it a step further?"

"Let's see," she said thoughtfully. "Do the right thing, in the right way. Disciplined."

"Discipled, disciple-inned?"

"Ha-ha."

"You know: the nun's rules, catechism class, even your father's well-meaning advice."

"Could be," she said. "Could be the story of my life. I'm getting sick of it, actually. Okay, tell me what's next?"

At first, I took her to mean the next topic but quickly realized she was referring to the whole course of our work together. "I'd like to follow you around some more. If that's okay."

"Of course it's okay. How else are you supposed to get to know me?"

"Thanks. I'd also like to get other people's impressions of you. I can't just depend on my own direct experience; I'm not that perceptive. Anyway, how would that be?"

"Perfectly fine."

"Great. Thanks for being easy about it. Then, in a few months, you and I will take a deep dive into the way you lead. Off-site. How about Sebago Lake? I know of a suitable place." She was agreeable.

Meanwhile, a Sit-Down with Sanjay

She arranged to meet with Sanjay as part of her continuing effort, nay struggle, to turn chaos into order. He insisted on going out for lunch even though the weather was bad—late November in New England. Against her better judgment, she agreed. In his early thirties, Sanjay already sported a paunch. Her eyes were helplessly drawn to it, the way people can't help noticing a deformity. *Disgusted* is not too strong a word.

He found a parking space across the street from the place, a busy street. As the light was changing, she dashed across. He waited for the next red light.

"Why do that!?" he said, as if shocked, concerned, and disapproving.

She brushed off his concern.

"Do you think you're invincible?"

"That's what my husband says," she said.

Sanjay just shook his head.

It was a sushi place. Inside, the tables were crowded together. Behind a counter, the Japanese chefs did their cleaving, folding, and arraying.

"I've never had sushi," she told him, hearing the foreboding in her own voice.

"No problem. There's other stuff, like tempura."

That is what she ordered. They were served quickly.

"Here, try one," he said. He adeptly chopsticked a small strip of tuna sashimi onto her plate.

Yikes, raw red flesh. She smothered it with soy sauce and layered it like a mummy with ginger. She fumbled with the chopsticks—hated that. Finally got it in her mouth. "Not bad," she said.

"Maguro—entry-level sushi," he explained. He was gratified that she'd tried it.

Besides the tuna, he ordered eel, shumai, and sushi rolls, lined up like a small army. He talked with his mouth full. She was reminded of her grandparents' farm animals that it had been her chore in the summer to feed.

On the drive back, he turned to her. "Was there something you wanted to discuss?"

"Another time." The food had taken over the conversation. She swallowed her frustration.

That evening, her husband, Lance, took one look at her. "How about a martini?" It was eons since they'd drunk martinis. They lived with their year-old doodle on the second floor of a duplex in Belmont, a leafy street. He was an assistant fencing coach at Harvard.

"What's Sanjay doing now?" he asked.

"It's not what he's doing. It's what he's not doing."

"Why don't you give him a piece of your mind? Parry, Veri. Thrust."

"That's a thought."

"Say something to that Neal guy. He's the one who got you into this mess."

"Poor, poor pitiful me," she sang, channeling Linda Ronstadt.

It took two weeks to get back on Sanjay's calendar, only to have him cancel at the last minute. They were able to meet a couple of days later. He chose a small conference room referred to as the fishbowl. One wall was a window.

Dispensing with his usual small talk, he said, "Okay, Veri, what do you have in mind?"

She matched his abruptness. "Performance management."

"What! Forced rankings, cut the bottom ten percent every year! Over my dead body. No way people in my company are going to be treated that way." He was talking about a practice that had started at GE. At first, it compels managers to remove below-par people, "deadwood." But if everyone is high grade, then it defeats the purpose.

"Not forced rankings! Why jump to that conclusion? I simply want people evaluated and paid in an objective and organized way. It's what grown-up businesses do." She went into detail.

Not one to interrupt, he heard her out. Process raised the dark specter of bureaucracy, ominous as midnight in a bad neighborhood. Entrepreneurs are allergic to process. Truth be told, they don't want it imposed on themselves. They are not about to be tied down, hemmed in. The best he could manage by way of a response was, "Okay, I'll think about it."

"Okay," she answered with an air of resignation like a senior in high school handed an unwanted curfew. She knew it was pointless to press her case.

She started having nightmares. One was recurring. She was riding her bike in Utah and fell into a slot canyon. A rock broke loose and pinned her right arm to the wall. There was no way to free it. And no one knew where she was; she had broken her mother's cardinal rule. When she saw the movie based on a book, *Between a Rock and a Hard Place*, about what had actually happened to Aron Ralston, an adventurer who climbed Colorado fourteeners in the winter by himself, she couldn't watch the part where Ralston does the gruesome bloody work of extracting his arm. Excruciating. She got out of her seat and pressed herself against a wall: *There but for the grace of God go I.*

One Saturday morning, as she and Lance were getting dressed, he quipped, "Restful night's sleep?"

"Yeah, right."

"Why don't you call it quits?" he said.

"I'm not a quitter. You know that."

"A challenge junkie from way back. But there comes a time."

"Our stock options haven't vested yet. And I've got this Sebago thing coming up. Maybe it will help."

The Off-Site

I chose a place I'd been to, Migis Lodge, a tasteful, rustic place right on the shore, knotty pine walls, a picture window facing the lake. It was off-season; we pretty much had the place to ourselves.

By her side, a bottle of Diet Coke. She had brought a supply. I handed her a black Moleskine notebook, unlined. "To deposit important bits. You'll never remember it all."

She didn't flinch as we catalogued her weak points. "No surprises," she said.

That's what they all say, but I let it pass.

We turned to her good points. She seemed unmoved. I decided not to probe and instead said, "Shall we turn—or return—to the subject of Sanjay?"

She didn't object.

"Question: After a meeting with him, what feeling do you come away with?"

"Can we step outside? I'd like some fresh air." She walked out to the end of a pier and balanced on the edge of it, then pirouetted around to face me. I was astonished.

"Were you a dancer?"

"I was, through high school. I was actually good enough to make a citywide ballet troupe, classical ballet. I didn't care for the looser forms, modern dance, jazz dance. I wanted to turn professional, but that was a pipe dream."

Back in the meeting room, she didn't miss a beat. "When I leave a meeting with him? Confused, maybe. I'm not really sure."

I didn't think she was being evasive. More likely, she had a lid on it, hers to open. "'Don't know' is always a good answer, especially when it's true."

She looked relieved. "Okay, let me think." A few moments later, she mouthed, "Shitty." So that I could hear: "Yuk."

"The yuk feeling—why would that be?"

"Yeah, why would that be?" She flipped open the black Moleskine journal I'd given her earlier. Her pen stayed poised above the page. She looked pained, gestured empty-handed.

"That's okay. Let's come at it another way. Are you and Sanjay at the same level?"

"No, not at all. On the organization chart, he's shown as reporting to me. But in real life, it's the opposite." To demonstrate, she stood up and tilted her arms so steeply I was afraid she'd tip over.

"That stance leaves you where? Just to put a point on it," I said.

"One down. I understand that. Face it: Sanjay is MobileAdTech. MobileAdTech is Sanjay. What gets me, though, is he takes advantage of his position."

I asked for an example.

"He does his emails in my staff meetings." Frustration rippled off her like radiant heat.

"Have you said anything?" That's the question: Will she suffer in silence?

"No. He should know better."

"Nothing you can do about it?"

"No." She was adamant, indignant, righteous.

"Prepare to be amazed," I proclaimed. "I've come up with a new tool. It measures a person's screw-you instinct. Is yours strong, weak, or somewhere in between?"

"Weak. I put up with a lot."

"How about stepping outside with your journal? This is a pivotal moment."

"Fine. I want to mention something first." She recounted the slot-canyon dream.

"Women who don't take up their power have nightmares. That's what the eminent psychologist Rollo May found in his patients. The title of his book is apt: *Power and Innocence*."

"That's me. But thanks to Sanjay, I might just lose my innocence—in this sense." With that, she went outside.

On her return, I asked if she would mind reading aloud what she had written. She had expected it to be a private conversation with herself—I didn't tell her otherwise—but she agreed. After looking at it for a minute, she exclaimed, "Holy shit! This is revelatory. I act like I'm, like, small. I act like I'm helpless. I'm fucking done with that."

"I congratulate you on your clarity. I congratulate you on your conviction. You're putting your foot down."

"It's true. I'm revolted. I will revolt."

She couldn't wait to tell Lance.

"Isn't that what I've been telling you to do?" he said.

That deflated her, and she couldn't hide it.

He changed his tune. "I was skeptical that Sebago business would do you any good. But I see you've got something out of it."

"The point is, it's *me*. I am part of the problem," Veri said.

"Sorry, I don't buy that. He's the problem, whether he means to be or not. We'll see. I believe in you, but I have my doubts about him, grave doubts."

"Deal. We'll see."

Turning Over a New Leaf

Back at work, she wasted no time in arranging a meeting with Sanjay. He was twenty minutes late. She did her best to eat her agitation, but when he mumbled a weak excuse, she went after him. "You're on your device in my staff meetings. Constantly fiddling with it."

He was taken aback. "Hey, I've got a lot on me, right? Besides, I'm listening. Try me sometime: I can repeat whatever's been said."

Surprising herself, she was inflamed. "You're missing the point. It's a lack of respect. You're the founder; you're supposed to set an example—a good one."

"But it was never my intention to be disrespectful, right?" He was oblivious as wood.

"Sure, and the road to where is paved with good intentions?" she said.

"Okay, okay," he replied, holding up his arms in surrender. "I'll do better."

She was all set to tell him he was like a Mexican jumping bean, constantly squirming in his chair, distracting her, distracting everyone. Consent was the last thing she expected. "You mean it?"

He nodded, his morality in plain view.

She was doubly pleased. Now she could call him on it in meetings. Disapproving as Mother Superior, she would.

"Lunchtime," Sanjay declared and rose from his chair. It was just then being laid out on the long table, from a local delicatessen. She helped herself to a small salad and a hardboiled egg. He'd piled his plate high with lunch meat and French fries drowned in ketchup. Meaning no harm, he remarked, "Veri, you eat like a bird."

"I suppose," she responded, thinking, *You eat like a pig!*

"How do you manage it?"

"Don't get me wrong. I enjoy food. My husband and I go to nice restaurants all the time. It's just that I stop when I'm full. Plus, I'm a glutton for exercise."

"Speaking of exercise," he began, then spoke at length about his brush with rock climbing. "We had to, quote, scramble up to a ledge that we'd then climb from there. Just being up there, on that ledge, made me incredibly uneasy. The whole time, I longed to be back on solid ground. I kept looking down at it, wistfully."

"Yeah, my athlete husband's like that."

"Oh, what about you—ever done any rock climbing?"

He was polite enough to ask but too self-centered to inquire early enough. He had no idea she was adventurous, a natural risk-taker. It wasn't just rock climbing. On hilly, twisting roads she drove her 4 Series BMW too fast. Skiing, the same story. Lance called her a speed demon. "Yeah, I've climbed a couple of times."

They dumped their disposable plates and utensils and sat back down. Having gotten somewhere on getting on his device in meetings, she thought, *What the hell?* and brought up performance management again.

He made a face. "Process: ugh. Veri, before you're done, you're going to strangle the company's entrepreneurial spirit, right? It's visceral with me, like fear of heights."

"Don't you see it's still the Wild West around here?" she insisted. "The way you operate, you'll never be able to scale. Want to know the truth? A year plus into the mission, I've gotten nowhere."

"Nowhere?" he protested. "The top team has regular meetings; it never did before."

"Yeah, that's one puny example. Name another one."

He couldn't.

"Want to make it two?"

"What do you have in mind?" he said uncertainly.

"What I've proposed: annual evaluations, which get you lots of things."

"Like what?"

She took a breath. "Like I've told you, Sanjay, employees know where they stand, they know how they need to improve. They get paid equitably. And, yes, the bad apples are removed from the barrel."

He took a deep breath. "Okay, okay, as long as you promise it will be done with a minimum of red tape."

She promised.

For him, it was a big departure. Gone was his ability to hand out salary increases or withhold them as the spirit—or whim—moved him.

I caught up with Sanjay a few days later. He freely admitted he'd dragged his feet. He knew he was being, well, childish, even sensed, dimly, that he was taking advantage of the situation. Moreover, treating people with respect mattered to him. It was another one of the company's stated values.

After several months of reasonably clear sailing, Veri judged the time right to bring up the "big one" and set up another meeting with him.

"Don't you look terrific today?" Sanjay told her as they sat down, coffee in hand.

"Well, thank you." She accepted the compliment, knowing he meant well. "Sanjay, in the name of full transparency—" Transparency was another one of the company's official values.

"What is it, Veri? Just come out with it." His impatience leaked out like sweat.

"It's your unicorn fixation." As an early entrant in the mobile ad space, the company had done very well. In just three years, its major product enjoyed a sixty percent market share, and the company had raised $95 million. Although it had yet to break even, the company was valued at $280 million. Yet Sanjay was not satisfied. In fact, he was overmastered by desire to attain "unicorn" status, a valuation of $1 billion, the ultimate measure of success in the start-up world at that time.

"My what?"

"You know very well what I mean. Your fixation isn't just bad for the company. It's bad for you." He started to object, but she held up her hand. "Sanjay, kudos to you for raising all that money—$100 million, for goodness' sake." She paused for a moment, for dramatic effect. "But it's gone to your head." She was polite about it but deadly serious. "You seem to think that big piles of money make MobileAdTech the next Google or Amazon."

He went over to the credenza and scooped out a fistful of nuts and berries. "I don't disagree," he said, munching away. "But, see, I've got a high-risk profile. Just starting this company was a big risk, right?"

She granted him that.

"Do you know what my first name means in Sanskrit? 'Triumphant.'"

"Well, in Latin, my first name means truth. I've got to tell you, I'm worried. We push out a product—hurray—but is the product ready? We're just chasing revenue. And we're taking too many longshots, and then if you don't see an immediate uptick in revenue, it's onto something else. There's no rigor. There's no discipline. And it's all driven by you."

"Look, Veri, I've got my heart set on this, on making this play."
She couldn't know he had a chip on his shoulder as heavy as a
plank. He told me several years later about a painful moment in
his life. He was in graduate school in the United States and overheard a couple of fellow students refer to him jokingly as "Black
Cherry." Hurt and offended, he made a bitter vow: *I'll show them
what a dark face can do.*

"Yes, but—" she began, but now it was Sanjay who wouldn't
brook an interruption.

"My mind's made up. End of story." He excused himself and
took the bowl of gorp with him, which did not go unnoticed.

That evening, she called Neal. "Your reasoning is sound, Veri,"
he said in a measured way. "And I give you credit for taking him
on."

"And?"

"For your information, I personally put in long hours trying to
walk him back. No dice."

"Can't the full board assert itself?"

"The board's timidity embarrasses me."

"So nothing can be done?"

"He owns fifty-one percent of the stock." Sanjay amounted to
a monarch. Ultimately, his actions could not be blocked, checked,
overturned. Not unless he broke the law, which he didn't do.

"That slipped my mind. How stupid of me!"

"Take it easy on yourself. You're new to the start-up world—capital structure and all that."

Off the call, she laid into herself anyway. *Why didn't you check
with Neal first? What must he think of you?*

Back to Sebago Lake

A few months later—it was a year and a half into her term—Veri and I were back at Sebago Lake. People told me she had made strides. Having learned to assert herself with Sanjay, she had begun to put her thumbprint on the company. "She has come out of her shell," Sanjay reported. Even though it made his life difficult, he respected her for standing up to him. Having dished out a large serving of praise, I looked at her expectantly.

"Thank you," she said graciously. Her face betrayed no feeling.

"That's it?"

"Well, what would you like me to say?"

She gave off an air of propriety. Was she being the obedient child? "Doesn't seem like all that good stuff made much of an impression." My tone was light.

"My mind is a sieve when it comes to compliments."

"What if you cupped it in your hand, retained it?"

"That's a novel idea," Veri said, and, at my suggestion, she went outside, to the end of the pier. The ripples on the lake caught her eye, the lake's great expanse. The moment was ripe for a revelation.

Returning to the meeting room, she told me, "You're right: If I held onto it, if I didn't let it slip from my grasp, I'd feel a lot better about myself."

"You say 'if.'"

"Because it's wrong to revel in my achievements," she said.

"Where did you get that idea?"

"My father, for sure. The moment I'd gloat over my grades or anything else I excelled at, he'd shut me down. 'Don't let it go to your head,' he told me all the time."

"Humility, a strong force. Can you push it aside for a moment and feel good about the gains you've made? Shut your eyes. I bet you can do it," I said.

After a moment, she said, with light in her eyes, "Yup, I did it, and, yup, good feeling seeped in." She made notes in her journal. "I can tell you this: I'm sick and tired of trying to be perfect." Like a sudden squall, scorn swept across her face.

"The takeaway?" I asked.

"I'm plenty good enough. How about that?"

I nodded approvingly.

She emblazoned it in red lipstick on her bathroom mirror, where it stayed for years, smudged yet legible. Mornings, she recited it like a benediction.

The Finish Line Gets Closer

In the meantime, Sanjay's bubble burst. He had been summoned to New York by his biggest investor. "Get your act together, Sanjay," he was told. "Until then, not a cent more." That was it for driving up the valuation by raising more and more money. Sanjay was forced to come down to Earth.

Veri had a bone to pick with him and didn't know that, humbled, he might be more pliable. She asked me to sit in on their meeting. To prepare, I arranged to talk with Sanjay first. He was quick to admit his faults.

"I've never been organized," he said. "I've battled that my whole career. It drives my wife nuts." It was disarming, endearing.

He freely confessed, a bit like a thief who turns himself in after he steals something.

"What were your study habits like?" I thought to ask.

"Terrible. I was always last minute. And I only worked hard at subjects I liked. The rest, I did just enough to get by." His lower leg bounced like a metronome. "I got As and Ds, even flunked once."

"Fair to say you're no good at making yourself do stuff you don't care about?"

"That's the long and short of it."

"What can Veri do?" I had no idea what he'd say.

"Stop acting like I'm the enemy." Clearly, he was hurt.

At their meeting, Veri went first. "Sanjay, as you know because you were part of it, the company adopted a product-development process, effective January 1." It wasn't just a way to tighten things operationally. It was meant to limit—if not strip—Sanjay's authority to issue new features unilaterally.

"And I've disregarded it, right?"

"Right. You come up with a bright idea, and, up to your old tricks, you tell the engineers to get to work on it. And they do. Of course they do."

"Guilty as charged," he said.

"Don't you see? We have to stop throwing money around."

"Veri, did you hear what Sanjay just said?" I asked.

"No. What?"

"I agree with you," Sanjay said. "I vow to abide by the approval process. Veri, I want us in the black as much as you do."

What he didn't say is he had a year to get the company into the black, couldn't bring himself to say it. But shortly afterward, Neal told her.

Vindicated! she said to herself and raised a fist in triumph. In a fit of inspiration, she decided to swim across Sebago Lake. Sensibly, she chose the narrow end, down by Jumby Bay, which was two miles across. On the theory you can always run or swim twice the distance that you practice, she swam a mile three times a week for several weeks.

"No way," Lance said when he heard she planned to do the two-mile swim unaccompanied. "I'll be in a rowboat nearby." She scowled but didn't say anything. When the day came, the lake was flat as glass, the sunny day smiling like God above. With a half-mile to go, she tired and her form began to fall apart. Lance tossed her a float and a nutrition bar. Refreshed, she finished strong.

A Letdown

She returned to work to find that Sanjay's thoroughly good intentions had already faded like bright-colored cloth exposed to the sun. She called me, upset, and asked to meet that weekend.

She drove down from Boston. We met for lunch at the Boathouse, in Central Park. It was mild weather, and the wall of windows giving out to the pond was thrown open.

"What will you do?" I asked after she explained the situation.

"Confront him. What else?" She was steamed up.

"You're certainly well within your rights."

"What are you hinting at?"

"Choices abound, that's all. Let me ask you this: What do you expect to come of it, taking him on?"

"All I know is he made a commitment. He can't just break it. It's the principle of the thing. Besides, I'd get the satisfaction from giving him a piece of my mind. That's more than I've managed to do with my own father, who, to this day, oppresses me with his free advice. But beyond that, I don't know."

She excused herself to go to the ladies' room. On the way, she admired the late nineteenth-century photographs of people strolling in the park and out on rowboats. On her return she said, "Tell me, is he trying to thwart me?"

"What do you think?"

"I don't think so. He's not a malicious person."

After lunch, she went off for a while, wanted time to think. We agreed to meet by the toy sailboat pond across the way.

About an hour later, she walked up, exhilarated. "I couldn't get in the water dressed like this, so I got on the water—rowed around the pond. It felt great. Okay, what if I confront him?"

"What will come of it?" I asked. "More to the point: Will he change his ways? Unlikely, highly unlikely. You know, this latest thing—on again, off again—it's like he can't help himself. He's culpable, and yet he's innocent. Does that make any sense?"

"Lots."

She got out her journal and scribbled away. Finished, she looked up, good feeling collecting on her face, her eyes limpid as rainwater. "When I get him to agree to something, it seems like he means it. Actually, he does mean it. But face it, he will stray. It's predictable, isn't it? He's the founder; he came up with the idea. He's got a controlling interest. He's not officially the CEO, but he's still the most powerful figure in the company. So there's a limit to what can be done with him—by me, by anyone. Even if he commits to something in good faith, he will stray—may stray. Especially if it goes against the grain.

"So where does that leave me?" she continued. "Here's where: If he's a sheep that wanders off, that makes me the sheep dog—or the shepherd—that nudges the animal, so to speak, back into line. Tries to. I won't stop trying to herd him back; I learned that lesson well, not to leave power on the table. But face it, sheep will get lost, which is really too bad. But, as my dad would say, it's nothing to get excited about."

PROLOGUE

Gideon is in line to be CEO and wants the job in the worst way. Any day now, the decision will be handed down. On the day of reckoning, will he be judged worthy?

JUDGMENT DAY

Gideon was startled when Corson barged into his office, waving a note Gideon had just sent him.

"You gotta get off my back, Gideon," said Corson, a program manager responsible for multiple projects. He had complained before about Gideon's strict rules and harsh criticism, but never with guns blazing.

Gideon had a terrible urge to strike back. But, mastering himself, just barely, he motioned to a chair across from his desk.

"What's got you so worked up, Corson?"

"It's that god-awful tracking system of yours. You put projects under a microscope. Trivialities, Gideon. Nickel shit."

"I'll keep that in mind," said Gideon, trying to keep the peace.

"Sure you will."

The insolence got to Gideon, but he kept his mouth shut, reminding himself, *In the end we'll be judged by our Maker.*

As Corson turned to leave, he said, "There are plenty more like me, but I'm probably the only one who will tell you to your face."

An image of his son Michael hopping mad at him flashed through Gideon's mind. *Where is he anyway?* Gideon thought, disapprovingly. *Elizabeth does a much better job of staying in touch, especially with her mother.*

Straight out of the Rhode Island School of Design, Gideon had been hired by a nationally prominent architecture firm. Like most self-respecting professionals, architects typically have no desire to be a manager. They are actually prejudiced against that type of work. But from the get-go, Gideon wanted to advance.

Conscientious, he worked punishingly long hours. He kept tabs on every construction project. On his return from a trip, he made himself read all the back issues of the *Wall Street Journal.* He tried to, anyway. The pile on his credenza kept getting higher. His heart sank when it caught his eye.

Travel, out of sight of his wife, Deborah, was also a chance to indulge his weakness for beef. Steak for dinner every night, French fries. Cheesecake for dessert. "Cholesterol abuse," a colleague had quipped.

Gideon treasured Deborah, was grateful beyond measure he had found her. She exuded genuine concern for others. She was understanding about his long hours, the importance of his career to him. "You'll see," he told her. "When I make it to the top, our life will be perfect."

He had risen to second in command, overseeing both commercial and residential projects, and was being considered for the top job. The founder-CEO was about to step down. Gideon would know in a week.

Usually behind on his sleep, he set two alarms to make sure. It wasn't the marital bed he slept in. Deborah had told him, "If you really think it's necessary to work that late and get up that early, I'd appreciate it if you used the other bedroom." He understood: No need to disturb her sleep twice.

For his crushing regimen, he could thank his father, who had drummed into his head "Whatever you do, do with all your might." Following his father's example, Gideon was also a devout member of the Church of Jesus Christ of Latter-Day Saints. He wasn't bothered that everyone called him a Mormon. He had met Deborah when they both attended BYU.

Like all faithful males in his church, he had served as an elder since he was eighteen. He subscribed to the doctrine that not just his actions but his words, thoughts, feelings, and desires would be judged, that records would be kept. God required his kingdom to be pure. If any part of him rankled at the tight moral regimen, the feeling never made it into words. His motto was *Do the right thing in the right way.*

His mother also deserved credit for his robust work ethic. On an ideal early summer day, just after his middle school got out, Gideon had mowed the lawn, using a push mower, no less. He'd dutifully raked up the clippings with the minute care his father required. Finally done with the tiresome chore, he flopped down on the lush, fragrant grass. *Ah,* he said to himself, *that feels good.* He thrilled to the sharply blue sky, viewed through the splay of newly leafed branches. But his mother, ever watchful, burst out of the house, the screen door slamming behind her. Rushing up to him, she sputtered in his face, "No son of mine will lay out in the sun doing nothing." He rose to his feet reluctantly. "Make it snappy," she said.

It was not lost on Gideon that his parents named him after a famous avenging man in the Bible, a faithful servant Paul mentioned in the book of Hebrews. As recounted in the book of Judges, Gideon was a military leader who led 300 men to a crushing victory over 135,000 Midianites.

Deborah had elected to stay home with the children and was grateful that Gideon made enough money for that to be an option. She'd been an elementary school teacher, a good one, for nearly a decade. As rewarding as that was, she didn't mind trading a classroom full of little kids for her own children.

She and Gideon had divided labor sharply. Divide and conquer, he'd said. But that meant they had very little time together, just the two of them. Except for an occasional flicker, romance had gone out of their lives. By now, the kids were grown and out of the house, but their relationship remained utilitarian. It had been a very different story when they'd first met. On the occasional date night, they did derive an almost sensual pleasure from a good meal, *ooh*ing and *ah*ing over each course.

With Gideon tied up so much, Deborah had learned to be independent. She assisted on research projects at the Citizens Committee for Children, became a docent at the Metropolitan Museum of Art, quite a feat. Gideon was her biggest fan. Every once in a while, he joined the crowd as she went over the finer points of German Expressionist paintings.

A Day of Rest

The day before the fateful decision, they had a Sabbath brunch at home after church. While Deborah cleaned up, Gideon stayed at the table, weighing himself against every criterion for the top job. "Geez, there's so much riding on this," he told her.

Completely out of character, she stamped her foot, startling him. "As if I didn't know! It's all you can talk about. I detest that place." The words fairly exploded from her mouth.

Gideon was stunned. "Detest—that bad? I had no idea."

"Of course you didn't."

"But hasn't the place been very good to us?" he said.

She waved that aside. "Have you ever thought about therapy?"

"Me? You've got to be kidding." Counseling was fine for other people. In fact, at church, he did quite a bit of it, pastoral counseling. He had a lot of energy for aiding people in their spiritual struggles.

"But we were able to send the kids to private school, the best one in the area. And look at where we live."

"You can justify it all you want," she said. "It's out of whack. Way out of whack."

"Don't we have to make sacrifices in life?"

"Would you please get off it, Gideon? You're trying my patience."

"I can't do anything right."

"Neither can I." She took a deep breath and let it out in a whoosh. "I let this build up and now the dam's burst." She managed a tentative smile. "Here, let's have a hug."

Judgment Day Arrives

He slept badly. *For Pete's sake,* he complained to himself, *I may not spend great gobs of time with the kids, but I really care about them, and*

I step in when it's needed; she knows that. Has she forgotten how devoted I am to her?

It took both alarms to wake him. Weighed down by exhaustion, he stumbled into the bathroom and took a cold shower. That wasn't unusual. The panic was. Today of all days, he had to get his head clear. Still groggy after the shower, he slapped himself on the cheek so hard it left fingerprints. But that did the trick. A little thought stole in: *What's wrong with you, beating yourself up like this?* A disturbance had broken out in the corner of his mind.

He toweled off and waited for the full-length mirror to clear so he could shave. From the fog emerged the image of a tall, handsome man, posture good, a full head of hair. But the flab around his middle commanded his attention. *Deborah must be disgusted*, he thought. *Forget Deborah: I'm disgusted!*

Pulling out of his garage in Morristown precisely at 6:00 a.m. to beat the traffic into the city, he thought, *Judgment Day.*

"Listen, Gideon," the CEO, Milton, said the moment they sat down in his office. "The board and I appreciate everything you've done for the firm, but at the end of the day, we don't think you're a good fit for the top job. And to be perfectly frank, there's room for improvement in your current role. I can go into detail another time." With that, he rose from his chair and patted Gideon on the shoulder.

Back in his office, Gideon slumped over in his chair and, for long minutes, held his face in his hands. He had never felt worse in his life.

On impulse, he moved to one of the guest chairs opposite and took in the view from that angle. *Where would the firm be without that guy over there, the guardian of quality? He's* the *one who caught the problem with the lobby ceiling in the Mass Ave office tower. The architect was too damned concerned with aesthetics. For God's sake, she hadn't left enough room for the A/C ducts. That guy over there, what if the Mandarin Oriental's fire-egress requirements weren't met; what if he hadn't caught that problem?*

Like a superb hunting dog, Deborah detected the heavy scent of disappointment. He put on a brave face. "They've decided to go outside," he said.

Hugging him, she whispered in his ear, "Gideon, you're a good man. That doesn't change one bit."

His daughter had come over for dinner. Generally stoic like her father, she surprised him by crying quietly, her arms around his neck.

That night, as he lay in bed, unable to fall asleep, his friend Bo came to mind. Bo was for Hobart, a consultant type. He and Bo knew each other through their wives. They belonged to the same book club and had brought the two couples together for dinner two or three times a year. The guys took to each other and started meeting on their own. Deborah approved. She thought Hobart, as she preferred to call him, could do her husband some good. Maybe he should call Bo. But that would have to wait 'til after the holidays.

New Year, Old Gideon

Early January, time for his annual all-hands meeting. He gazed out at the 200 people seated in the auditorium. "Folks, today I'll stress Gideon's rule number 3: no unbudgeted work. Try to slip an overrun by the client, good chance we get caught. They scream bloody murder, we have egg on our face, and we eat the cost. Get a change order!"

He took in the audience, looking people in the eye. "It's not just the money. It's our integrity, not to be trifled with." Gideon didn't mind playing hardball. It's about doing the right thing, even if that meant going over time sheets with a fine-tooth comb. He cited examples and took questions; there weren't many. He couldn't help noticing that not everyone looked his way. Corson made a show of it.

He and Bo had a favorite hangout, Scallywags, an old-fashioned Irish pub in Hell's Kitchen, photos of James Joyce, William Yeats, Samuel Beckett, and George Bernard Shaw on the wall. Gideon always had a lot on his mind, and Bo had fallen into the role of listener, sounding board. Bo ordered a pint of Guinness, Gideon a nonalcoholic beer. Gideon told him about being passed over.

"Your reaction," Bo said, "is only natural and yet—is all that upset okay with you? I mean, does any part of you object to it?"

"It's not just the promotion, Bo," Gideon said. "The day before, Deborah really let me have it."

"That doesn't sound like her. What got her so upset?"

"My job. She says it dominates my life; she's sick of it. She's felt that way for years."

He was lost in a hellish reverie when a waitress, new to the place, walked up. He had noticed her, a pretty, red-haired young woman with that milk-white complexion common to the Irish.

"Another round, guys?" She smiled at him warmly. His heart swelled. *God, I could fall in love with her.*

No question Gideon was faithful to his wife. His conscience

usually didn't permit him even to look at other women. But he had not succeeded in repressing his appetite for the feminine form, discretely outlined in the young woman in front of him. Deborah had obscured hers by putting on a little weight, pound by stealthy pound. When he traveled, he permitted himself to take in a sexy R-rated foreign film. This sort of thing, tasteful stuff, was racy enough for Gideon.

Bo brought him back to the present. "Weren't you going to follow up with the CEO? What's his name again?"

"Milton. I postponed it." He grimaced. "If there's one thing I hate, it's people sitting in judgment of me. But, yes, I did get around to it. Milton held the meeting at the University Club. Old-money stately. Shows you how seriously he took it," Gideon said, brightening a bit. "He'd actually talked to people on my staff, plus a smattering of first-line architects. Told me first. Did his best to be impartial, I heard."

Bo broke in. "Impartial? Really?"

"I do think he wanted to be helpful. Still, what he told me stung. No way it wouldn't."

"Specifically?"

"I'm too negative. Always hunting for what's wrong. You're guilty until proven innocent. Never an encouraging word. People still respect me, but this thing takes a bite out of that. A big bite."

"Anything else worth mentioning?"

"Unfortunately, yes. That I'm righteous, opinionated, even 'sanctimonious.' And when I know what's right or think I do, it's hard to get me off it."

"Yeah, we've had our share of arguments, haven't we?"

"Well, you may feel what other people feel—that I'm insufferable."

"Insufferable? I wouldn't say that."

"Thanks for siding with me, unbiased person that you are. But you don't work for me."

"So where do you come out on all this?"

"I come out of it feeling lousy about myself. It got me thinking about myself as a father. A dust-up with my Michael sprang to mind. This is when he was fifteen, sixteen. I'd pay him to wash and wax my car, pretty new at the time. I'd take a look when he finished. A close look, I'll admit. This particular time, he had done a pretty good job, as usual, but I found a couple of places he'd missed.

"With fire in his eyes," Gideon continued, "Michael threw down the buffing cloth and walked off. Hot under my collar myself, I caught up with him inside. 'Hey, you've got to learn to do things the right way.' I viewed it as one of my august duties as a father, imparting that value. When Michael left a spot here or there, I read it as a moral lapse.

"'Find somebody else to harass,' he shot back. We made up later, but he never did my car again. I said to myself, *That's okay. I'm preparing him for life. Someday they'll look back and appreciate what I did for them.* But now I'm thinking I made a mess of that too. Here's a crazy idea: You could talk with them. Privately. They both know you, Fourth of July picnics and such."

"It's not crazy. On occasion, I interview family members. But I'll only give you themes. Why not have me talk with Deborah also?"

"Her I've heard from! Just the kids for now."

Bo Interviews the Children

Bo called Michael first.

"Really?" Michael said. "You're not going to repeat any of this to my father?"

"That's the understanding. You can count on me to stick to it."

"Okay, I'll do it. Might be good to get this stuff off my chest." Michael didn't mince words. "I hated my dad. For the way he drove us and drove us and drove us. That and the rough way he disciplined us."

"An example?" Bo asked.

Michael hesitated. "This is not something I've ever talked with anyone about, outside our family. A slap across the face. Discipline was never mild."

"How long did that sort of thing go on?"

"Into my teens."

"Did you ever speak of this to your dad?"

"It crossed my mind, but he wouldn't have taken it well. I didn't trust myself either. It might have ended badly."

Elizabeth told Bo, "Michael's the sensitive one; he exaggerates." But her account squared with his. "When I was out of line, Dad gave me a good whack on the behind," she said. "Michael, being a boy, got it worse than me. Maybe he wasn't exaggerating. But it wasn't cruel; it was controlled. And instructional. It always came with a lesson."

With a smirk, she added, "We could have done without the lesson. I can forgive him for all that," Elizabeth said, "but he refuses to meet my boyfriend, who's Black."

"As his friend, all I can say is give him a chance. He may come around."

"I wish. I enlisted the aid of my aunt, his sister, and she got nowhere."

Bo had known Gideon laid down the law with his kids. But the corporal punishment shocked him. At first, Bo chalked it up to fatigue. He knew Gideon played tired. But he told himself, *Don't make excuses for him.*

Gideon and Bo Connect Again

Back at Scallywags, Gideon thanked Bo for talking with his kids. "They both made a point of telling me they enjoyed it. Therapeutic, even. And with a little prompting, they each told me that, on balance, I had been a good father, but it was no picnic." He paused. "For a change, Deborah and I went away for the weekend. Out to Bridgehampton. It's beautiful there in the offseason. I bared my soul like I've never done before. Remember when she was royally pissed off at me? I got down on my knees to ask for forgiveness, but she wouldn't have it.

"So I did the next best thing: I confessed. I told her, 'I've always believed in family first, but I didn't practice it worth a darn.' She said it was big of me to say that. I told her I wanted to start living by that principle. 'Isn't it a little late?' she said in a kind way. But saint that she is, she was just great about it all. Funny thing: That conversation and the time away brought us closer than we've been for ages." He swelled with good feeling, a brimming pool of it.

But nights were difficult for him. Still sleeping alone, he couldn't stop kicking himself. *How could you treat your own kids so badly? How could you let your wife down like that? And in the name of what?!* He'd turn from side to side like a pancake flipped in a hot pan. The thrashing around would have disturbed Deborah's sleep if they shared a bed.

Enter the Therapist

Deborah got wind of his distress, and over his objections—"I can solve my own problems"—she fairly dragged him to her therapist.

Mathew Zhang, slim, balding, with a soothing voice, told Gideon he was Taoist. "The Chinese character for 'crisis' is made up of two other characters." Zhang scooted over beside Gideon. "Problem," he said and made heavy, dark marks. "Opportunity," he said and drew faint, wispy lines.

"Is this the way it's usually drawn?" Gideon asked. "Because one is much more pronounced than the other."

"Precisely," the therapist said.

Deborah smiled.

"Precisely what?" Gideon said, impatiently. *What is this Eastern mystical bullshit?*

Deborah's smile vanished. She reached over and touched Gideon on the shoulder, as if to say, give the guy a chance.

He took a breath, and it came to him. "Ah, I see. You wrote it as I've been feeling it."

The therapist nodded with something short of complete satisfaction. "Which is what way?"

"I've seen my present situation as mainly a problem. A problem with me. The opportunity part—well, I haven't scratched it."

Saying nothing, Mathew drew the two-part character correctly.

Pointing to it, Gideon said, "There's my challenge—to cool it with the breast-beating and go for the upside."

"Yes, to live life in the correct proportions." Zhang began kneading Gideon's shoulders from behind.

Gideon jerked back, thrusting Mathew's hands off. Thinking, *Next thing, this guy will have my clothes off,* he told Deborah, "Let's go," and went into the anteroom for their coats. "Deborah, you didn't tell me this was part of the deal."

She stayed silent.

They were both quiet on the car ride back. He wanted an apology, and she was not about to offer one. It was a weekday afternoon. He was not going to go back to the office. She offered to make tea. She sat on the couch, he in the nearby chair. They talked pleasantries, and then Deborah said, "Apart from his laying hands on you, I thought it went well."

"Yeah, I don't disagree. But what is Taoism anyway?"

"Well, it's about balancing yin and yang. Yin being the receptive principle, yang the active principle."

"So he's trying to get me to ease up on the active principle and ease into the receptive principle?"

"Yes, I believe that's what he was doing. You've never had a massage?"

"A stranger laying hands, as you say, on me? No way."

"What if I did the massaging?"

"That's an entirely different matter."

"No time like the present. C'mon." They went upstairs to their bedroom. One thing led to another.

Over dinner, she said, "I'd like you to go back to Mathew. And if he massages you—fully clothed, of course—no big deal, okay?"

He took a deep breath. "Okay."

Return Visit to the Therapist

"Good to see you both again," Mathew said.

Gideon nodded.

"Have you tried mindfulness?" Mathew asked.

"What in God's name is that?"

"Relaxing your mind. Here's a way to do it. Make a fist."

Reluctantly, Gideon did, with his right hand.

"Good. Now clench it, hard, and close your eyes while you're doing it."

Gideon went along.

"Hold it . . . Hold it. Release. Do you feel a tingling in your hand?"

He did.

"Okay, now your lower arm."

The relaxation exercise took about fifteen minutes.

"Okay, when you're ready, open your eyes."

They stuck a little. Despite himself, Gideon smiled a little. "It worked." Deborah reached over and squeezed Gideon's thigh.

"Did anything go through your mind?" Mathew asked.

"Yeah, well, I beat myself up. I've been such a screw-up at work and at home."

"Do you think you deserve a beating?"

"Probably. Deborah, isn't that the way my mind works—punish, be punished?"

"Pretty much," she said.

"Boy, am I screwed up," Gideon said, scowling.

"Are you punishing yourself over that?" Michael said.

"It's ingrained. What am I supposed to do about it?"

"According to the Buddhists, the root of all suffering is expectations, which can be changed."

"That's a thought." Gideon asked whether there were ways to relax his mind. He chose TM, transcendental meditation, despite its name. He liked the formality of it and the idea of a mantra.

The next day, he stopped by the finance head's office. "Lucas," he said, "I've got an assignment for Fernando."

"What could you possibly want the controller to do?"

"I want him to take over the scrutiny of time sheets and to prepare invoices personally. I see now it's below my pay grade."

"It's below his pay grade too. Why not give that to someone on Fernando's staff?"

"Two reasons. One: Getting billing right is key to the firm's credibility. And two: It's a responsibility that's hard for me to part with, overseeing it. I know I can count on Fernando."

"Fair enough," said Lucas. "What if he wants to talk to you about it?"

"Fine, just send him my way." Shaking Lucas's hand, he said, "Really appreciate it." That was better, he told himself afterward. *I'm on my way.* As experiences like this mounted up, he discovered he rather liked being likeable. *I don't think I'm any less effective either.*

He told Bo, who said, "Surprise, surprise: Harmony isn't incompatible with accountability."

New Rules

Gideon's annual rules meeting rolled around. He welcomed everyone. Milton the CEO was there too, which was unusual. Gideon began by announcing a new rule. "Catch someone doing something right." That caused a stir. He surprised everyone further by reciting the previous years' accomplishments. Good news had never been part of the program.

"What's come over him?" people whispered.

Gideon's nemesis, Corson, said, loud enough for those around him to hear, "This too shall pass."

Tongue firmly in cheek, Gideon said, "I know you'd all be disappointed if I didn't, per usual, go over the rules."

"Right," someone said in everyone's hearing, "a crushing disappointment." There was laughter.

My God, Gideon thought, *they're with me.*

"In place of that, Milton and I have instituted an Employee of the Year award. Actually, three each year." Gideon's idea. Milton handed out the awards, a certificate of appreciation and dinner for two at a just-opened and favorably reviewed Danny Meyer restaurant in Battery Park. Everyone clapped enthusiastically. The CEO, out of character, gave Gideon a high five.

"Well done," he said. Naturally, it was a good feeling, but it was a different good feeling.

Later that year, Gideon gave Bo a call. "I think I'm doing better. But what do other people think? This time I'll pay you."

"Out of your pocket?" Bo asked.

Gideon nodded.

"Keep your money."

It took Bo several weeks to make the rounds; it was a busy period for him. The two of them met in Bo's office; this wasn't a social occasion. "You think you've changed," Bo began. "Other people think you've changed too. End of story."

"Wait a minute," Gideon said, taking him seriously. "Specifics, I need specifics."

"Down, boy. One: You're down-to-earth, off of your high horse. Related to that, you're not acting like a judge as much."

Gideon broke in. "Yeah, 'judgmental' came up another time."

"Probably me who said it. Okay, three: You're more relaxed. Quote: 'more comfortable with himself.'"

"It's true, but how can they tell?"

"Apparently, it shows. To your kids too. One of them said you're no longer so invested in their careers. 'More detached,' as one of them put it. Interesting: Coworkers picked up on that too: 'Gideon used to be almost too proud of his children's accomplishments.'"

"Ego." He scrunched up his face.

"Everyone's ego leaks. Welcome to the club."

"All these years, I've thought of myself as the big helper, the great giving volunteer. Was that just a sly way of feeding my ego?"

"Tell me now, is there such a thing as pure altruism?"

"I guess not. What gets me, though, is that this despicable

selfish need has had its way with me. And all along I thought I was in control!"

"Who was it that said the mind is a cracked mirror—Spinoza?" Bo said, "Wait a minute. Weren't we validating you? How did we get off of that?"

"Easy in my hands. Let me get something off my chest. I'm afraid that, come Judgment Day, there will be too many black marks on my record."

"Heavy, heavy. I see you're not out of the woods yet."

Meanwhile, Back at the Pub

The following Saturday, Scallywags again. Bo ordered a draft Guinness, and Gideon, in a mood to indulge himself, had an urge to follow suit but refrained.

"Bo, I want you to know I'm coming around."

Bo nodded, as if prepared to be impressed.

"The warts are ugly, but they're mine." They both had a good laugh over that. "You'll love this, Bo. I used to structure my Saturdays like a day at work. I had to have a full slate, laid out hour by hour."

"That's whacko, Gideon. You're a whack job!"

Gideon didn't mind the ribbing. "Yeah, I was like a drill sergeant to myself. But lately, I got myself to relax the Saturday schedule, go with the flow, as Deborah says. There's that word again: relax. So now I free myself up by noon or 1:00 and take Deborah to lunch. She prefers that to brunch. We go to Café Luxembourg. Do you know the place? Corner of Amsterdam and 70th. Then we go to an art museum or gallery, an opening that weekend. I tell her, 'You lead; I'll follow.'

"But it's not all peaches and cream. I'm still judgmental. Yeah, I know, everyone's judgmental, but this is serious." Long pause. "Elizabeth has a Black boyfriend. She wants us to meet him. I refused. Deborah is on me about it. Mind you, she's been good about it. Hasn't gone to the mat."

"Want to talk it over?" asked Bo.

"Not really. This is between me and my Maker."

Elizabeth and her boyfriend went to different schools—she to Villanova, he to Penn—but they had met in a hiking club that drew from colleges in the Philly area. The club took day trips to the Poconos. The two of them had ended up sitting beside each other on the bus, and they hit it off.

To Elizabeth, it was no big deal that Frank wasn't White. But she knew her father, not the most open-minded person in the world, would look at the mere fact of Frank's race through different eyes. That's why she wanted her parents to meet him. Frank was handsome, intelligent, personable. She knew her mother would take to him immediately. Her father, well, he'd be impressed that Frank went to an Ivy League college—not only that, the Wharton School of Business at Penn.

The following Saturday, Gideon and Deborah again went to Café Luxembourg for lunch, to be followed by a docent-guided tour of a new exhibition at the Met. After they'd eaten, Deborah reached for his hand and said, "Let's talk about the boyfriend. Okay?"

Gideon didn't want to but didn't object.

"Well, I took the train to Philly last Tuesday, and Elizabeth introduced me. I didn't tell you in advance; I didn't think you'd approve, and I felt I owed it to Elizabeth. Anyway, the three of us had coffee together. He made a good impression. Clearly, they're fond of each other, but they weren't falling all over each other the way some young couples do. There's no reason not to meet him. No good reason." She stopped there and looked into his eyes. It was an invitation as much as a challenge.

He went to the restroom and took a long look at himself in the mirror. He didn't like what he saw: a middle-aged White guy who couldn't get with the modern world.

"Okay, I'll meet him. I owe it to you; I owe it to Elizabeth." He felt good about himself for flexing.

Deborah gave his hand a strong squeeze. "Good for you. I'll let Elizabeth know. Better yet, you call her."

"Yes, but I want them to sleep in separate bedrooms."

"Not to worry," she said, with a gleam in her eye. "They'd only come up for the day."

She's laughing at me, he thought. *I deserve it.*

Another Tête-à-Tête with Bo

The following Saturday, Bo and Gideon were back at that Irish bar. It was the first warmish spring day. All over the city, restaurant tables had sprouted up on sidewalks like dandelions. The two of them sat outside. Except for the occasional bus or siren going by, it wasn't hard to hear. The traffic on 9th Avenue is light on the weekend. Gideon couldn't wait to tell Bo about the boyfriend breakthrough.

Bo clapped his hands like he'd just taken in an intoxicating performance. "Quite the growing guy, aren't you?"

Gideon would later discover Bo had sent Deborah a text on

the sly. She had been waiting nearby, and in a New York minute, she stepped out of an Uber and walked up to them, beaming. She had slimmed down, and so had Gideon; they had done it together. Looking not a bit matronly now, she was wearing a straight skirt, fashionable that season, with a black sweater adorned with a pearl necklace. She looked great; clearly, Bo could tell it wasn't lost on Gideon, who rose to greet her with a big smile on his face and surprise in his voice: "What are you doing here?!"

Bo pulled over a chair for her from a neighboring table.

"Hello, Hobart!" she said, greeting him warmly. "What have I missed?"

They both caught her up. She just listened, nodding and smiling at points. She called over a waitress, who happened to be the very same young, red-headed one from Gideon and Bo's previous visit, and ordered something in a low voice. Gideon wondered what was going on.

The waitress returned in a few minutes with champagne glasses and a bottle of nonalcoholic effervescent wine. Then, attracting a bit of attention from people seated at neighboring tables and even passersby, Deborah stood up and raised her flute. The two men rose and did the same. Beaming, she turned to her husband. "I'm so proud of you, Gideon."

She reached into her largish bag and, with a grand gesture, placed two plane tickets on the round café table. "To Barcelona!" she announced, joy written all over her face. "Gideon and I are going on a second honeymoon," she told Bo. "Aren't we, Gideon?"

Actually, he had brought up the idea of taking a trip, just the two of them, to celebrate their twenty-fifth anniversary. But she'd obviously decided to take matters into her own hands.

"I hear May is an ideal time of year to go there; nothing like Barcelona in fine weather," said Gideon.

Taking him by surprise, Deborah leaned over and kissed him squarely on the mouth.

PROLOGUE

Maxine, off the charts smart and a favorite of the CEO, has a rude awakening. Her issue runs deep. Can she fathom it?

THE EXPERT
WHO GRINNED

Maxine Cooper was the brainy CEO's intellectual pal. He liked to brag that she had a PhD in materials science from MIT. It was no surprise that he put her on a much-ballyhooed task force to stay abreast of technical advances.

"I'm proud of you," her husband, Teddy, said when she told him over dinner. Her teenaged daughter, Justine, who thought the world of her mother, followed suit. Maxine asked Justine about her weekend homework. Justine made a face but complied. Her father, a natural-born harmonizer, soon changed the subject.

The company made diagnostic equipment, MRI machines, X-ray machines, CAT scanners, retina scanners, AI-enabled dermatascopes, and the like. The company also serviced its products, a second line of business. The head of that line of business invited Maxine to present a preview of the task force's findings to his team after just a few months.

Maxine was happy to oblige. "We've heard a lot about the Fourth Industrial Revolution," she began, "but how did the Industrial

Revolution get started in the first place?" She always sought to understand the present against the sweep of history. "It really took off with the steam engine, which was a lot more productive, obviously, and a lot more reliable, obviously, than wind power, water power, horsepower, human power." This was the first time she had presented to a team at this level, and she was nervous. Still, she smiled a little as she spoke.

"The spinning wheel was foot powered and equipped with just a single spindle. With the advent of steam power, spinning machines soon boasted ten, fifteen, twenty spindles. Same story for weaving. Productivity went through the roof."

Someone looked down. It was as if she were praying. Actually, she was on her handheld device. Someone else was looking out the window.

Oblivious, Maxine added a bit of social commentary: "There was no mastermind behind the Industrial Revolution, no guiding hand. Does anyone know when the Industrial Revolution began?" One person raised his hand; Maxine didn't notice. "The 1760s. Anyone know where it started? England. Why England of all places? Not just because the wool trade had long flourished there, but because England liberalized its economy. And that was a consequence of the Glorious Revolution of 1688, which clipped the royalty's wings. No longer could kings appropriate private property at will. Property rights gave entrepreneurs a big incentive to innovate."

The segment president spoke up: ""Maxine, this is all very interesting, but can you jump to the punch line?" He gave the eye to the people, now two of them, on their devices.

"Oh, sorry." She sped up, practically out of breath, tripping on her words. "Quickly, the Second Industrial Revolution—mass production—was made possible by precision tooling and inter-changeable parts. This was the late 1800s, by which time England had lost its technological lead to Germany. If I had more time, I'd tell you why."

"Max, please," her boss broke in. "The Fourth Revolution, where it's taking us?"

"Where it's taking us," she recited as if she were trying to grasp an obscure notion. "Okay, I'll skip the Third Revolution, the com-puter age, happening in your own lifetimes, blossoming at your feet. But take a look at this." She held up a cylinder of pure silicon. It gleamed like metal but not quite. "A semiconductor. It's produced in a clean room and sliced into wafers, silicon wafers. What inte-grated circuits are mounted on." She was as excited as a child doing show-and-tell. "Sorry, I couldn't help myself."

"We noticed," the services president said, indulgently.

"Okay, finally, the Fourth Industrial Revolution: artificial intelli-gence, AI." She had everyone's attention now. "Sensors coupled with robots will usher in a world almost entirely controlled by machines. Sensors that are designed into the machines. Sensors that trigger maintenance, itself automated, before equipment breaks down. Sensors that prompt supplies to be reordered automatically when inventory runs low.

"That's now. That's machine learning, which is just highly sophisti-cated number crunching. Yet it's nothing to sneeze at. It beat the chess champion of the world, Gary Kasparov. But it is nothing compared to what's coming next: AGI—artificial general intelligence, machines that think like we do. Robots that reproduce themselves, that write their own code. The end of civilization as we know it. Scratch that. When will this happen? Here's a photo of Broadway in 1905. How many cars do you see? Only one. It's hard to pick it out in a street clogged with horses and horse-drawn carriages. Here's a photo of Broadway just twelve years later. How many horses can you spot? Just three amongst all the cars. That's how quickly. Except quicker because the pace of innovation has sped up."

"Services, Max." Her boss, the CTO for products, stepped in.

"In the near term, thanks to sensors that will be built into our scopes, technicians will know the condition of every piece of customer equipment all the time—remotely. That means faster and higher-quality maintenance.

"Down the road? Technician in a box. AI-enabled scopes won't need an expert to teach doctors and other medical personnel how to use them. The built-in expert system will do that. Glitches? These scopes will be self-healing. Tech services? Gone, like the airline people who used to check us in and take our baggage, replaced by kiosks."

"That's good for now," the services executive said.

In the end, Maxine's audience couldn't help being impressed with her mastery of the subject; nor could they help feeling that much of the time she was talking to herself.

Time to Choose the Chief Digital Officer

Not only did the CEO make the task force's recommendations a top priority, but he also created a new position, Chief Digital Officer. Thanks to Maxine's intellectual firepower and her ability to master practically anything—and quickly—she was a candidate. Naturally, it helped too that she was already conversant in IT. She had educated herself in it just for her own satisfaction. She knew data analytics, kept up with cybersecurity, could write code in two languages.

But the company decided to go outside.

"Listen, Maxine, the company is lucky to have you," the company's HR head told her on a Friday. "I mean that. Not getting this job, you can look at it as a failure. Maybe there's no escaping that, but—"

She broke in. "I don't get it. I know that space like the back of my hand." Maxine wondered whether being a woman was a factor. "Was the CEO in on this?" she asked.

He was.

Okay, she thought, *the deck was probably not stacked against me.*

"You can look at this as a chance to raise your game," said the HR leader.

"Raise my game—what does that mean?"

"You've never done 360 work, have you?"

She shook her head no.

"Well, I suggest you do. I'll make a consultant available to you, Simon Whitman. He's worked with other senior people here. Are you game?"

"I suppose." *What choice do I have?* thought Maxine.

She left work early and yelled her head off in the car. "Screw it!" she bellowed, whacking the top of the steering wheel. "Screw it, screw it, screw it!" In the garage, she cleared her next week's schedule. *I could give a shit.*

She sprinted upstairs and left her work clothes where they fell, like dropped banana peels, and put on her running togs. Spurning the trails in the nearby heavily wooded park, she crashed through the woods straight uphill. She swish-kicked her running shoes through piles of dead leaves like a kid. A branch scratched her cheek; she hardly noticed. She fell when a root caught her toe, but she got right back up. Tired, she kept going. When she reached the top, she threw herself down on a grassy spot bathed by the sun and rolled onto her back. In minutes, she was asleep. A chill woke her an hour later. Clouds had moved in. She got to her feet and let out a great beast-like groan. For the moment, she had achieved peace in body and soul.

She walked in the back door, leaves stuck to her back and legs. Her husband, Teddy, gave her a look but only said, "Home early?" It was Friday; she always chose the wine for dinner. Not tonight.

Halfway through dinner, Justine turned to her: "*Maman, tu es très silente. Es-tu malade?*" Justine took French, and Maxine had lived in France.

"*Non, je ne suis pas malade.* I had a hard day at work; that's all." Justine searched her mother's face and seemed satisfied.

While Teddy loaded the dishwasher, Maxine went upstairs and straight to bed. She skipped her nighttime routine completely. From the bookcase, she plucked a title she'd long intended to read, Proust's *Remembrance of Things Past*. In French. She heard Teddy's footsteps on the stairs but they retreated. *You're done, finished, kaput,* she thought and turned off the light.

Up early and clad in a bathrobe, she padded barefoot down the carpeted stairs and pressed the red power button on the coffee maker; Teddy ground fresh coffee every night before turning in. Her mood wasn't quite as dark as the coffee, which she took black. Cradling the mug with both hands, she stepped out on the back porch. The early autumn day was expected to be mild; a last-gasp bloom on the clematis caught her eye. Her spirits rose a little.

Teddy found her lying on the living room couch. A high school English teacher, he had high standards of his own, but had a hard time relating to her high-octane work life. "How are you this morning?" Normally, she'd be at her desk by now.

"Crashing, that's all." That's all she'd say. The rock star in the family, she had an image to uphold.

Midmorning, Justine came flying downstairs in her pajamas and went straight to her mother, worry on her unblemished face. "Mom, how are you? Are you better today?"

Maxine tried to reassure her.

Justine nodded and went straight to her father.

"Give her a few days," said Teddy. "She'll be fine."

All morning, Maxine lay on the couch, absorbed in the Proust book: *It's as mopey as I am.* Went outside to the chaise longue as it got warmer. She smiled at the clematis vine.

Teddy kept her supplied with lemonade. Not too many ice cubes, thank you very much. Justine came by twice and kissed her mother on the cheek. It was the sort of thing Maxine herself was given to do with her child. Justine came by again and, this time, squeezed in next to her on the couch. They were not big people.

"What are you reading?" she said, gently tugging the book away. "Which page are you on—point." She read a few pages and handed the book back. "Good writer. Not my speed." As she got to her feet, she reached for her mother's hand. "Maman, let's go for a walk."

Maxine was not so dispirited that she couldn't accept that rare invitation.

On Sunday evening, Teddy suggested they play gin rummy, a pastime usually reserved for vacations. She did not indulge the perverse impulse to turn him down. Teddy had a run of good luck. The next game, she got gin but discarded too quickly. She went to the bathroom, not to use the facilities but to recover. She wasn't sure which was worse, losing the hand or screwing up.

Monday morning, her assistant called. Some appointments couldn't be canceled or moved. Reluctantly, Maxine agreed to take them by phone. She made herself thank the assistant.

After dinner, she suggested playing cards again. This time, she went on a winning streak of her own.

Every time she got gin or won a game, Teddy said, "Good for you."

She frankly couldn't comprehend being happy for your opponent when they won. As Teddy was busy making tea for them, she recalled a story often told about him when he was a little kid. He'd been playing Chutes and Ladders with his mother, and just as he was about to win, he said, "You win, Mommy."

He returned with steaming mugs. "Okay, Maxine, tell me what's up? You've had the weekend."

Yeah, to lick my wounds. "I didn't get the promotion." She didn't mention the "help" she'd been offered.

Later that evening, Teddy took Justine aside. "Your mother had her heart set on a big job. It would have meant working together with the top guy."

Maxine practiced piano all week, Bach's Goldberg Variations, a notoriously difficult piece. It helped keep her mind off her troubles. On Thursday evening, Teddy found her on the couch, sitting longways, reading Proust, the third volume. "Get anything for you?"

"No, I'm good. Can I tell you something?" She pulled up her legs to make room for him.

He hesitated when he heard "tell."

"I've been watching tendrils."

"Watching what?"

"Ten-drils," she said, drawing out the syllables. "On the clematis out back."

"Yes, and what have you observed?"

"There was just one thing, actually," she said, "the way it lengthened and strained to secure itself to something higher. This time, there was nothing there."

"Interesting," he said with all the sincerity he could muster and got to his feet.

"Darwin," she continued, patting the cushion where he'd been sitting, "studied tendrils too."

He sat back down.

"Like me, it was during, shall we say, a confinement. He had a climbing plant placed at the foot of his bed and observed the tendrils at work. This was right after his daughter, Alice, died. Ten years old. He took it very hard."

Teddy nodded and stood up again to walk away.

"Teddy," she called out. "Darwin actually wrote a little book on tendrils that I was able to locate. I read it this week. *On the Movement and Habits of Climbing Plants.* Thanks for listening."

Halfway down the hall, he turned and said over his shoulder, "You're welcome."

The Consultant Reaches Out to Her

On Friday, her boss, the CTO of the products segment, phoned her. An engineer and a creative type too, he was friendly as usual. "How are you doing, Maxine?"

"Just fine, thanks." She was friendly back.

"Enjoying your week off?"

"Very much, thanks. I needed the break. Hardly did any work."

"Good for you. It's so easy to get sucked in. I'm overdue for a vacation myself. See you Monday?"

She answered yes.

"By the way, that consultant, Simon, will get in touch next week. Take care."

On that Monday, Simon Whitman called. He introduced himself as a "guide."

"Guide: That's a new one on me."

"Yeah, in my case, 'guide' is, uh, more descriptive. You'll see. Question: What do you want out of this?"

"I don't know. This wasn't my idea," she said.

He tried something else. "Have you ever worked on yourself with help?"

"Never. I haven't avoided it. It just hasn't come up. Has the need arisen? That would be your next question, right?"

He didn't say anything.

"Yeah, I suppose it has." She had talked herself into it.

Just before Christmas, the CEO called. "Hey, Max, wishing you good holidays. And, listen, this IndRev stuff is great, but all it amounts to is optimizing the space we're already in. I want you to give some thought to a broader play. What might that look like?"

"Good holidays to you too," she said brightly. "Yeah, glad to. How long do I have?" End of January, he said, and signed off. That call shot her spirits into the stratosphere: She still mattered. And what a delicious prospect, to get futuristic.

She read widely over the holidays and called a two-hour meeting of her team for the first week of January. Still in high spirits, she welcomed everyone and told them what the CEO wanted. "What do you think? Here's my thought," she said. "We deal in diagnostic equipment. Why not treatment equipment? Not passive stuff like stents or sutures. Active stuff like pacemakers. They don't just set a floor on a person's heart rate; they monitor it remotely. Or hearing aids. Medical fixes, an adjacency the company could easily move into. It's a growing market, old people."

"Seniors, Max," her HR person broke in.

"What?" She made a face. She didn't care for euphemisms.

A recent hire, fresh out of engineering school, jumped in. "Yeah, what about equipping a dermatoscope with a laser for zapping basal cells—or squamous cells; that is, if they don't need to be sliced out?"

"Now we're talking!" she said.

"Doesn't have to be electronic," a man with a PhD in biomechanics said. "Serious burns, for example. Bioengineered fixes for that."

"Yeah, burns that require more than a skin graft," Maxine said, taking the ball out of his hands. He sagged back in his seat. "Skin grafts won't take without an underlayer, a dermal matrix, that forms a wound bed for the graft. That can be made of natural or artificial materials. How would we get FDA approval? Would we classify it as medical equipment or medication?" So it went, Maxine holding forth with evident pleasure, a big smile on her face.

She briefed the CEO. The door was closed, as it was for all of his meetings. For the first time, she was conscious of an ineffable male–female aspect to their interplay. *Is he making a play for me? Nah, just enjoy it.*

January was eventful. Simon called to say he'd finished collecting data; he was ready to brief her. She suggested they meet in her office. He countered: too many distractions. They settled on an out-of-the-way conference room on another floor of her building. When she arrived, he was rolling four of the six swivel chairs away from the table. With a team, he preferred to get the table out of the way completely.

"Which do you want first?" he asked. "The good things or the problem areas?"

"Spare me the good things," she said. The words leapt out of her mouth. *What are you, a masochist?*

"Do you want the punch line, or would you rather go through the data and come to your own conclusions?"

"The punch line."

"Okay. Maxine, you're like a big bright light. In and of itself, that's admirable, that's marvelous, that's enviable, right? In and of itself. But there are other people out there. What does, uh, that make them? A lesser light, right?"

Gulp. "Fine poetry, I suppose. Can you put it in simple, practical terms?"

"Yes. I asked everyone to split 100 points between your tendency to talk versus your tendency to listen. It's close to seventy–thirty, talking to listening."

My God, she thought.

"You had no idea?"

"No. Look, I'm busy getting to the bottom of problems. I'm busy ferreting out solutions. I mean, that's my job, isn't it?"

"You're caught up in the 'what.' But the 'how,' not so much?"

"I never thought of it that way. But what difference does it make? Do you have numbers on that?"

"Now that you mention it, I do. Do people come away from a meeting with you with more energy or less energy? What do you think?"

Uh-oh. She opened her mouth to speak, then closed it.

He waited.

It was a standoff between her competitive urge to guess and her dread of the answer. Silence not her forte, finally she broke it. "Less."

"Less. Ten of the fifteen people I interviewed said less."

She sighed with a great rise and fall of her chest.

"Perhaps a bit of comic relief?" He reached for a book under his pad of paper. "This is from a memoir by Gabrielle Hamilton, a restauranteur and quite the writer too. She says about her sister, 'Her purpose in telling a story isn't so much to tell a story. Her purpose is to take a long luxurious bath in my ear and disgorge the entire contents of her brain.'"

He laughed; she did too, grateful for a little fun, even at her expense. But that abruptly gave way to dismay. *You, the walking encyclopedia, you're nothing but a big blind spot. Pathetic.*

They stepped outside for a breath of fresh air. "Hey, you're forgiven," said Simon. "It's your nature. Like water carried by a Roman aqueduct. Gravity's the pump."

"*L'acqua della conoscenza è pura.*" Her eyes twinkled.

"What?"

"The water of knowledge is pure."

They had a little laugh. When they'd sat down again, Simon said, "You've got great mastery, and you've got great fluency. Really impressive powers."

"Powers. My father once told me, 'True happiness is using your powers fully.' I remember the moment: I had just told him with evident pleasure that I'd aced the calculus final." Her drive to mastery had always thrilled him. Was his involvement unhealthy? Probably not. It was a vector into inborn forces that carried her in that direction anyway.

"That's neat, really neat. To that point, do you realize that, as the words come pouring out, you smile?"

"A shit-eating grin?"

"That's harsh. So you didn't know?"

"No, I didn't. Another blind spot. You know so much! I had no idea I was taking private pleasure in public, to put it crudely." She blushed.

"Embarrassment aside—." A beat late, he saw he didn't have her attention. He waited, looking down at the table.

"'Don't suck all of the oxygen out of the tent.' My husband has been telling me that for twenty years."

Simon snort-laughed. "Oxygen: What does that stand for?"

"Beats me!" She started to smile and quickly crimped it. Now she was self-conscious about smiling. "To answer your question, it's what people need, to put their powers on display."

"You got it! There's one more thing," Simon said. "Can you stand it?"

She could.

"Okay, you've got, um, weak players on your team. Do you see how that fits the pattern?"

She did.

"Let me guess: You pick up the slack."

She did.

"Weak links demotivate strong links, which could be one reason why morale on your team isn't great."

She sighed, then noisily she ripped out a sheet of paper from the back of her pad and wrote: *LET IN THE LIGHT!* They clapped right hands in triumph. Suddenly, she had a fright. "What if the CEO saw this?" Meaning the report.

"He won't."

"But what would he think of me if he did?"

"I wouldn't worry about it. He's dazzled by what he sees. That's probably all that matters to him."

When Maxine curled herself around Teddy's back that night, a swirl of emotionally loaded thoughts kept her awake. *Who do you think you are anyway—Superwoman? No. But what's wrong with being me? Plenty. You're not a good leader, and you're going nowhere fast.*

Maxine Embarks

She made a good-faith effort to reform, but it was sidetracked after a few weeks by a circumstance in her personal life. Justine, now a junior in high school, was slacking off. One weekday evening, when Justine had been on her phone for an hour, Maxine couldn't take it any longer.

"What are you doing, Justine?"

"I'm texting my friends—anything wrong with that?"

"Nothing, up to a point. But on school nights?"

"Right, Mother," Justine said. She never used that form of address.

The next night, Maxine came by twice. Both times, Justine was hard at work. The third time, she was on the phone, but Maxine made herself walk away without saying anything.

Saturdays, the family went out to breakfast. It was almost always a pleasant thing. "Justine," her mother said as casually as she could, "you know how we have phone-free meals together? Like now. Well, Dad and I suggest carrying that over to school nights."

"You mean you and Dad won't use yours either?"

"Dad and I need it for our work; at least, I need it for mine. But in your case—"

"No."

Maxine turned helplessly to Teddy, who tried to make peace. "My dear daughter, your mother just wants the best for you."

"Yes, Dad, I know." Her mild tone matched his. "But when do I get to decide what's best for me?"

On her next call with Simon, Maxine brought it up. "Justine was dealt a good hand, everything you'd want and nothing you wouldn't want. I can't stand to see her misplay it."

"Is there a reason why she's not working as hard?"

"Yeah, her social life is taking off."

"Isn't that, uh, a good thing?"

"I get it. There's more to life than work."

Spring semester, Justine's grades matched the previous fall's except that two of her four As dropped to A– and the lone A– slipped to a B+. Teddy and Maxine didn't make an issue of it. They'd keep an eye on it in the fall. But that summer, an emotional fog descended on Maxine, which was pierced by a phone call from Simon. "I keep hearing you monopolize meetings."

"Yeah, I can't find the wand." When he asked if she meant a magic wand, she laughed. "No, the wand you use to open the blinds. You know, to let the light in."

"You can't contain yourself?"

She just sighed.

"How about placing yourself in an actual container?"

"Stop talking in riddles," she said, but she knew what he meant. She later hit on the idea of a review meeting, one that would be structured to minimize her role. It was time to follow up on an early-stage R&D initiative, a next-generation MRI machine, Maxine's brainchild. It would be a much faster and much smaller piece of equipment, one that didn't send the claustrophobic into a panic.

"Okay, gang, let's see how we're doing," Maxine said. She turned to her chief of staff, Cameron, who she had charged with running the meeting. He put up a slide with a list of action items, each shown in green, yellow, or red. The first item had a green next to it. Discussions with Siemens medical imaging business: Yes, they might want to partner on this.

"Any questions?" Cameron said, looking around the room. There were none.

"Well, I'm not so fortunate," said the next person, a senior technologist, whose action item, a cutting-edge imaging start-up that had originated at MIT, was marked red. "I don't like to make excuses, but this one is beyond my control."

"Meaning what?" Cameron said.

"The founder is impossible to deal with."

"What can I do to help?" Maxine asked.

"Call the guy, you and I."

"As soon as we're done. Better yet, let's jump on a plane, meet in person."

The meeting moved along swiftly. Acting mainly as a cheerleader, Maxine didn't have that much to say. She gloated, *What's so hard about changing?*

But outside of review meetings, Maxine still couldn't shut up. "Yeah, it's a long putt," Simon said. "What about a portable structure? You're a technologist; you'll come up with something."

It was the fall semester of Justine's senior year, and she was still not applying herself. It got to the point where Maxine, with Teddy's agreement, banned Justine's phone during certain weekday hours. Justine went along with it. But to her parents' surprise, she took to doing her homework at the kitchen table. Occasionally, the phone in the kitchen, a wired line—Maxine refused to get rid of it because the sound quality is better—would ring, and sometimes it was for Justine, just now filling out, her hair long. A boy, a classmate, had started calling on the pretext of going over homework.

One night, Maxine couldn't take it any longer and yanked the phone, with its long cord, out of Justine's hand. She yanked it back. It was a regular cat fight. Panting, they both let go of it at the same moment and it clunked on the floor. Her face scrunched up in pain, her heart pounding wildly, Maxine rushed out of the kitchen to find Teddy.

He hugged her. "What's wrong?"

She just shook her head and nuzzled deeper. Finally, breathing normally, she said, "I lost it with Justine," and slipped from his embrace.

That weekend, she asked her daughter to take a walk with her—a return to the wooded park, this time on the gravel path. "I have a proposal for you," Maxine said. "I'll stop being your supervisor. I'll be there for you if you want. How does that sound?"

"That sounds good, Mom."

They shook hands on the deal and hugged. Maxine's hopes shot up.

The following Tuesday evening, Justine stretched the curled phone cord into the pantry and shut the door. It was the same boy. Mustering self-control, Maxine made herself wait for twenty minutes, then knocked. No answer. Upset, she made herself wait ten more minutes and knocked again. Nothing. She wrenched the door open and lunged for the phone. This time, Justine just handed it to her and dropped her arms to her sides. By chance, Teddy walked into the kitchen and saw what happened.

"Maxine! What the hell?"

Justine hadn't moved. It was as if the evil queen had turned her to stone. Teddy took the phone and handed it back to Justine. She muttered something into it and started to cry. He patted her on the shoulder and followed Maxine up into the den. He, too, had high hopes for their daughter, but he didn't believe in interfering and rarely did. That was his stated policy, and he practiced it, to a fault sometimes.

"Listen," he said sternly. "This has got to stop. Your takeover tactics may work in the office, but they have no place—I repeat, no place—with our high-school-age daughter." He suggested she work in their bedroom on weekday evenings. There was a desk there. She had no objection. She had sinned; this was her penance.

On her own, she decided to absent herself from family councils. Didn't trust herself to take part. While Teddy and Justine talked things over, she sat herself at the top of the stairs. She was able to hear, and that was it. *Ridiculous, but that's all I'm capable of.*

Later that week, Teddy offered to play gin rummy—to soften the blow, she thought but jumped at the chance. It had just occurred to her that she could be happy for him when he won. But she lost, and her out-of-character impulse dried up like drops of perspiration on hot pavement.

At her next scheduled meeting with Simon, she opened with "You'll be proud of me. I came up with a portable structure: an egg-timer, the hourglass type."

"Great idea."

"But it didn't work. I'd forget to flip it over. But that's the nature of innovation: trial and error. I could cite examples—" It was a joke. "So I got myself a watch with a timer. It vibrates, noiselessly, and resets automatically."

"Brilliant."

"Listen to this." She read aloud, "'I had been meaning to reach out regarding the meeting. I thought you did a great job creating room for all voices. Thanks for your leadership there.' That's from a peer." She was silent for a minute, then blurted out, "Justine. I'm failing her."

He sympathized. "That's no fun! But why are her grades so important to you? Do you have any idea?"

"I'm her mother, for God's sake. I want all the doors of opportunity flung open to her."

"I can relate. I have kids of my own."

"Look. I've got colleagues who went to an Ivy League school, and years later, it still defines them."

"You didn't go to an Ivy League college, and you've done pretty well for yourself," he said, half joking.

She was unmoved.

"Maxine, tell me this: What stories got told about you as an infant, as a toddler? You know, your God-given nature before the world got its mitts on you."

"Well, my father was forever saying 'energy spilling over.' At dinner, I got giddy. Giggled, squirmed in my seat, poked my sister, kind of took over the room."

"Irrepressible?"

"That's a good word for it. To bleed off that excess energy, he introduced me to his stationary bike. This was later on, maybe eighth grade. I got on it every day, without fail. A real maniac. I still need heavy exercise. Much later, my dad had occasion to say about me as a kid, 'She wanted what she wanted.' That hasn't changed."

"How might that quality come into play with Justine?"

She made a face, then walked around the room like a predator trying to pick up the scent. "I want the best for her. What else would I want?"

"The river of one's actions usually has more than one tributary."

"Very poetic but what's it supposed to mean?"

He just grinned at her, devilishly.

"Are you implying that my love for Justine, which I've always thought of as a pure thing, is contaminated?" She looked like she'd just bitten off something rancid.

"Just that more than one thing could be going on," he said. "Why don't you sleep on it."

"That's what the French say: *la nuit porte conseil.* The night conveys wisdom."

They met for breakfast.

Maxine, looking refreshed, announced, "I talked with Teddy last night and he said, 'Of course, you're too invested—I could have told you that.' I suppose that's it: I love my kid too much. Or I'm living through her, trying to. And it's not working. Simon, I'm beginning to see the light."

"The guiding light," he said. "Good for you."

"Thanks. But it's like being pulled through a knot hole."

"True. It's not been easy. It almost never is. Here's one for you: the toughest self-analytic task is to see how one purchases self-esteem."

"Tough is the word, wrenching," she said. "The way a scientific revolution is wrenching. Like . . . like when Copernicus discovered we're not the center of the universe!"

PROLOGUE

Jim, whose family was struck by tragedy, must come to grips with its effect on him if he is to have the future he wants at work and at home.

ARM WRESTLING WITH MYSELF

I have a quarterly meeting with my team coming up, and I'm planning to do something I've never done before—get input. On myself. I've never had a coach, never gotten feedback. Bad attitude, I told myself.

I asked an internal consultant, Gretchen, who's very professional, very competent, to facilitate. She had helped me sort out the strategy for this business when I was put in charge of it three years ago, along with its capable eight-person team. I knew I'd be annoyed if the team didn't credit me for being responsible, highly responsible.

This got me thinking back to one particular day etched sharply in my memory. As always, my alarm was set for god-awful 4:45 am. As always, I bonked it quiet. As always, a monumental act of will that never ceased to surprise me pulled the covers aside. The shock of the cold air that morning propelled me into action. I was thirteen.

Throwing on my clothes, I shot out the door. I quickly folded the stack of newspapers that had been tossed on the curb and jammed them into the dirty gray bag that read *The Register* in red. Hoisting it over my shoulder, I pedaled away. It was a new English bike I'd bought with my own money.

Still dark, nobody out. A familiar scene I never got used to. I felt as exposed as a dinghy lost at sea. I made a game of flinging paper after paper Frisbee-like onto the front porches. I'd gotten good at it. Only once or twice most mornings did I have to retrieve a paper from the bushes or lawns. I'd learned to ease up on speed for better control. The misery of being utterly alone at night was relieved by just plain moving. That's always what I'd wanted at work: forward motion and a winning feeling. That's what I wanted from the feedback meeting with my team.

Quarterly Review

As usual, the quarterly meeting was off-site, this time in a walled-off section of a ballroom—banquet chairs, the two or three fake-wood tables covered with white tablecloths to make it look like a conference table, pitchers of water, small bowls of hard candy in wrappers.

I kicked the thing off. "Listen. I'd like to hear from you about how I lead, how I could lead better. Tell it to me straight. If it stings, fine. I don't have to tell you how important it is for all of us to keep getting better. Gretchen, over to you."

She knew most of the players from helping us with strategy and had introduced herself before we started to the two people she hadn't met. Other than that, she came into the meeting cold. She and I agreed to go on what people said firsthand.

"Thanks, Jim. Good to be with you all." With her ready smile, she had a way of putting everyone at ease, but you quickly took her seriously. "Would it be natural to go straight to what needs work?" People nodded their heads. She smiled and said, "But that's not what we're going to do. We're going to start with what's good."

"Hey, no need for that," I said.

"That's what they all say." She was having fun at my expense, but I didn't mind. "Let's do the complete job, shall we?" I couldn't argue with that. "You're not one to half-ass things, are you?"

"You got me there." I'm incapable of half-assing anything. "You're the professional. I'll follow your lead."

She handed out three-by-five cards and had everyone write down the three things they most appreciate about me. The sales guy, Vince, burly, bald, and outspoken, spoke first. "Lights-out bright, gets it right away. That's number one."

I interrupted. "I'm not so sure about that."

Gretchen none too subtly drew her hand across her neck and let Vince continue.

"I am," Vince said. "Two: broad shoulders. There's nothing he won't do; nothing's too difficult."

Gretchen interrupted. "Talk to Jim. He's right there."

"Okay. Third, you're a helluvan operator. You know how to get shit done."

The finance guy, Philippe, sharp as a tack but too sharp-edged with people, jumped in next. "Great at execution. We almost always hit our numbers. Knows the business like the back of his hand. And, holy cow, is he competitive—wants to win, wants the team to win."

"Philippe," I broke in, "I bet you're going to say to a fault."

This time, Gretchen didn't stop at gestures. "Jim, your job is to listen. Fly on the wall, okay?"

"Okay, I'll try to shut up."

Philippe had one more. "Oh, and he really cares about his family." I noticed Gretchen did not prompt him to readdress himself to me.

"That's four, but who's counting," Gretchen said. Three more people basically echoed what had come before.

"I'll go next," said Elizabeth, the tall, affable HR head, newly promoted to her role but not bashful. "If I had to pick one thing that defines you, Jim, it's heavy lifting. I'd also say caring; I mean that in the broad sense. You want employees to be treated well. It kills you to lay people off."

I couldn't resist. "In a broad sense, huh. That sounds like a veiled criticism."

Everyone looked at Gretchen for a reaction, but she gave no sign. The other three people offered more or less the same things. By the time everyone finished, my eyes were moist, much to my surprise and chagrin.

Recovering, I turned to Gretchen. "Now can we get to the stuff I can do something about?"

She had people turn their three-by-five cards over and write down three concerns. While they worked, she and I went out in the corridor to huddle. "I got emotional; could you tell?"

She nodded.

"It wasn't just their words; it was the sound of their voices—if that's not corny."

"Not at all. Anything else?"

"I was overcome with relief. Those are the things I want people to see in me, but—you never know."

Back in the room, Vince again went first, and everyone followed in the same order. I resolved to keep my mouth shut and actually sat on my hands. "Jim," he began, "I've got a strong personality, and I've met my match in you. It doesn't faze me, but not everyone grew up in a rough neighborhood in Queens. That's the main thing. An off-shoot of that: Anybody meeting with you, they better have their act together."

Philippe echoed that. "I'm not the cuddliest guy, but that's my job: to give people a hard time. But you, you can't just be hard-nosed if you want their hearts as well as their minds. The other thing: You shoulder too much of the load."

Someone said, "I second that motion" and went on much as Vince and Philippe had. After two more sets of similar comments, Elizabeth spoke up.

"Here's something that hasn't come up yet," she said. "Jim, you know so much—what a big brain—and it's all at your fingertips, but God help the person who isn't absolutely on top of a problem in their area. You get very impatient; some might say abrasive. I don't have to spell out the damage that does, do I?"

I shook my head no.

She continued, "Jim, your impatience comes out in another way: You jump in too quickly. You finish people's sentences." Looking Gretchen's way, she said, "I'm almost done."

"How many is that, Elizabeth? Ten?" Philippe said.

She sent him daggers and went on. "Jim, you've got great energy, but you're incredibly intense. I hope you don't mind me being blunt." She didn't stop being friendly, even when blunt.

When everyone had said their piece, I thanked them and said I'd get back to them soon. Gretchen had everyone hand me their cards, which I've kept to this day.

During drinks (as usual, there was an open bar) Gretchen took me aside. She was about to say something, but I couldn't contain myself: "Having to be on top of everything—that really hit home."

"Everything ends up on top of you," Gretchen said. "It's as if you carry the weight of the world on your shoulders."

"Interesting that you should put it that way. I identify with Atlas, who literally did that. Actually, in Greek mythology he was made to carry the heavens, not the Earth, for what that's worth."

"How did you come to be Atlas? If I may ask."

Usually, I kept my tale of woe to myself, but I decided to make an exception in her case. There was something about her (the light in her eyes, the way she met my gaze; I don't know what exactly) that led me, contrary to my nature, to trust her. Still, I didn't say what first came to me, which was that a meteor collided with my family's planet and extinguished much of life as I had known it. Instead, I fed her my stock answer.

"I lost my father at a tender age, so I had to grow up fast."

"Really!" She radiated compassion that I found genuine. "What happened? How old were you?"

"He died of a heart attack when I was thirteen."

"So a lot fell to you?"

A lot, I said. Evidently she could tell I didn't want to go into it further, because she quit asking questions. But just that brief exchange hit me hard. Crushing sadness.

Gretchen, very intuitive and understanding, sensed what was going on. "Did that mention of your dad take you back?"

I gave a little nod, sad and sentimental.

I was again being called upon to adjust, but this time I had to force it on myself. But did I really have to change? After all, I'd always had to be the best I could be, and I'd done pretty well for myself. Why change? Why tamper with a winning formula? For days, I vacillated.

The Day Lightning Struck

The day my father died, my school day had been interrupted in Miss Olive's seventh-grade English class. It was the period right after the lunch break. I'd wolfed down my sandwich and played baseball with the other guys. A minute late, I ran into the classroom, breathless and sweaty, and rushed to my seat, calling attention to myself halfway on purpose. She gave me a look but didn't say anything. She knew I worked hard in her class.

Miss Olive was young but stern, no nonsense. No way we middle schoolers got unruly in her class. "Of all the unmitigated gall," she'd say, hands on hips, to some smart-aleck comment. That day she'd had us diagram sentences. "Subject, predicate, direct object?" she'd ask, pointing to a word on the blackboard. Hands shot up in a whirl of adolescent energy. You wanted to be the first one to get it right.

Suddenly, the door opened, and the principal's assistant stuck her head in. "Jim, step outside, please," she had called out to me.

Disbelieving, I'd looked around. "You mean me?" The class buzzed like a hive of bees, thinking I was in trouble.

To my great surprise, my mother was standing in the hall. I

could tell from her face that something was wrong. She took me outside and hugged me. I pulled away to see her face. "What is it, Mom? What's wrong?"

She'd been crying. She kept crying and crying. She'd start to speak, but the sobbing blocked her. "Speak, Mom, speak." She reached for me again and buried her face in my shoulder. At that stage, we were the same height. If anything, I was a little taller.

Finally, she had stifled the sobs enough to whisper, "Dad had a heart attack."

"Is he okay; will he be okay?"

"He died on the spot." Her face fell apart like an egg cracking open.

"No, no, no!" I whirled away from her, leaned over, and threw up. I wiped my mouth with the back of my hand. She handed me a tissue. "How could he die of a heart attack? He's in great shape." My dad was athletic and only fifty-two.

"Yeah, it's so unexpected. The doctor said maybe a congenital heart defect. The medics didn't get there in time to revive him."

We went home, where she'd promptly poured herself a glass of wine, drank it, and then poured another. A blank look came over her face, her eyes open but seeming to see nothing.

We'd been used to her disappearing acts. Her eyes would defocus and stay that way for quite a while. "Mom's world," my sister and I called it, a grudging acceptance of something we couldn't do much about. She'd bite her nails, sometimes down to the quick, where a skinny line of blood would appear. At those times, she was good for nothing. My father would call to her, jostle her upper arm. She wasn't easy to rouse from her private reverie.

Later that evening, we'd found her sprawled on the couch, face down, puke splattered on the rug. "Disgusting," my sister said, sobbing, and ran out of the room. Breathing through my mouth, I wiped my mother's face with a moistened washcloth. I gently raised her head and slipped a clean hand towel under her head. It was really weird, me handling my mother like she was a child. Wrong. I felt good about doing what was needed, but I also felt deserted. I'd been deserted and suddenly made to be responsible like never before.

I later learned from my uncle, my father's older brother, that my mother had trouble being on her own. She'd been like a clematis vine that winds itself around a post or pillar. It thrives and flowers that way but if the supporting structure fails and falls, so does the plant.

Early Career

After college, I had started out as an engineer in a plant that made custom-designed electrical connectors, little plugs at the end of a wire. The work was interesting, I had a good boss, and I was paid well enough to send money to my mother every month. I threw myself into the job. I was consumed by the passion to excel. Before I knew it, I was put in charge of a team of engineers, many of them older than me.

The plant was located in a small Southern town. Not much to do there. I'd dated but wasn't ready for marriage. I liked living my own life outside of work as I pleased. I played in a fast-pitch softball league, joined a bowling league with people from work. In middle school, I'd been in a bowling club that played after school once a week—candlestick pins and a ball the size of a grapefruit. You played the deadwood; the pins weren't cleared. A grocery store job displaced both extracurriculars, and I didn't have the chance to get very good at them. Now I was bowling with big pins but not very good with them either, so I started practicing on my own. After a while, I got it into my head to bowl a perfect game, a 300, twelve strikes in a row. Very rare in those days, especially for a recreational bowler like me. The next season, I dropped out of the league to work on my game. I got very good, sometimes just a few strikes away from a 300.

The time I got the closest, I had entered the tenth frame only needing three more strikes. *Here's your big chance*, I said to myself. I made my usual several-step approach and released the ball, as I always did. The pins splashed apart, but there, in the right corner, stood the ten pin. Like Tantalus's apple, the prize stayed tantalizingly beyond my reach.

Something's in the way, I'd concluded. You've got your physical game down pat. Could it be your mental game? My first thought was no: I take a deep breath. I visualize. But, in fact, emotions, stealthy as a bandit, had been stealing my attention. Anytime I got within reach of a perfect game, I got giddy or panicky.

For some reason, I took to giving my head a slight shake, more like a shudder. But wonder of wonders, that little motion had chased away the small cloud of emotion that gathered in my head. Not long after that, I achieved my goal, but it was almost anticlimactic. Just as sweet was learning to control my emotion.

In my early thirties, I'd been transferred to Germany as head of engineering and manufacturing at our plant there. Mercedes,

BMW, and Audi were all customers. Working closely with each company, we engineered connectors for new models three or so years in advance and built them in time for the new model year.

In Germany, I had met another expat, Cristine, and promptly fell head over heels in love. I knew right away that we were a good match. We did such a good job of talking things through, getting on the same wavelength. We didn't work in the same department—she was in finance—so we rationalized it was okay to see each other. On weekends, we traveled all over Europe, either by car or train, to all the great cities: Barcelona, Prague, Vienna, London, and, of course, Paris. But the best part was that we synced up so well. She was transferred back to the States, and I arranged to follow. Back together, I proposed, and she accepted.

Coach B

The best man at my wedding had to be Coach B. He had stepped into my young life at its bleakest. I'd been forced to give up the baseball team and go to work. The season and the school year were almost over when Coach B called my mother and asked if he could drop by. I couldn't imagine why. He came over on a mid-May school night; it was still light outside. In front of me, he told my mother, "I want Jimmy on the summer team."

I was floored. The summer team was made up of players from the school team. "Can I, Mom!?" My voice was full of urgency and joy but she ignored me.

"He has to work full-time," she told Coach B. In her situation, money had mattered more than sports.

"He'll paint houses with me," Coach B said. "I'll pay him well."

That satisfied her, and she agreed. I quit my grocery store job that didn't pay much anyway.

Each summer, Coach B had picked one kid, a kind of protégé, to paint houses with him. He was a taskmaster, his standards exacting. The first week, we were up on ladders doing the second story. I figured, *Who's going to see it anyway?* and I skipped a spot here and there.

"That will never do," he told me on the first day. "Doesn't matter if no one ever sees it. It's our standard, and we will hew to it."

Slapping on paint with those wide brushes, we hadn't been quite side by side but close enough to talk as we worked. He talked a lot. That took getting used to. A big fellow who didn't stand on his authority, he read the newspaper and books, he watched sports, he saw films, and he told a good story. But unlike some talkers, he didn't go right on to the next thing. He wanted back-and-forth. He wanted to know what I thought. Finding the words was like trying to catch a bird in flight. So he'd draw me out.

My first week, the NBA finals were on. "How about last night's game?" he had asked.

"Good game." I was not easy to draw out.

"Yeah and what about it, would you say?"

I hadn't been prepared for that.

"Uh, it wasn't just the Michael Jordan show. The whole team was involved. That's what I like about their triangle offense. It took a long time for the team to learn it, but now it's another thing that makes them almost unstoppable." He had gotten me talking.

"I see you've followed the team closely!"

Coach B had me play shortstop. "That player is the infield leader. He has the most responsibility—calls pop-ups, lots of balls hit there."

Later on, he'd suggested I major in engineering. Mechanically inclined, I knew how to fix things. I had to, once my father died. At the wedding, I set aside time to be with him, shortly before the rehearsal dinner. I told him, "I never had a chance to thank you properly."

He waved that away. "It was the right thing to do, and you made the most of it—end of story. This morning I had a chance to chat with Cristine. Quite a gal."

Time was up, and he'd moved to hug me. It was only natural, but I had never hugged a man before. It just wasn't done in my family. But with him, I couldn't refuse, and I didn't.

Procrastinating

I was taking such a long time to get back to the team that Gretchen intervened. Her knock on the door to my office startled me. I'd been daydreaming. Beating her to the punch, I said. "I know. I know. I need to follow up with the team. But let me ask you something—I mean tell you something. Preceded by a question." I was all over the place. "They want me to throttle back, right?"

"That's one way to put it."

"So, if I gear down from 120 miles per hour, what's to keep me from dropping all the way to sixty? Me, a fast-lane guy."

"You're afraid of losing your edge?"

I told her yes, that was it exactly.

"Have you heard of cognitive behavioral therapy?" was her response.

"Spare me the psychobabble, Gretchen. Just tell me in plain language." She let it go, but I felt bad about it and apologized.

"That's okay. The idea is simple. Wrong beliefs, needless feelings." I saw how that applied to my concern of the moment. She went on. "Here's something, which was left unsaid at the off-site and may help you get off the dime. You're seen as arrogant."

"But I'm not. Quite the opposite."

"I don't see you that way either. But that's what some people make of you knowing everything and doing everything—and can't ever say, 'I don't know' or 'I made a mistake.'"

Gretchen did get me off the dime. My assistant organized a conference call with the team for the following week, Gretchen included.

"Thanks again," I said, "for telling it to me straight. Look. I get it. I'm too big. If I'm too big, what does that make you? It makes you smaller. That's criminal. Why put big people like you on my team only to cramp your style? No good reason. So, just as day follows night, my first goal is to let leaders lead."

I paused. In that brief opening, people piped up: "Makes sense," "Good for you," and the like.

"Another problem with being too big is I trample meetings, which brings me to—"

"'Trample,' that's too harsh," Elizabeth objected.

"Which brings me to my second goal: Let people finish."

"Makes total sense," Philippe said.

Vince added, "This is you at your attack-the-ball best." Then he surprised me with, "I better get after my own faults."

As I was about to end the call, Gretchen said, "Hold on. Aren't we—you too, Jim—falling right back into the usual pattern? It's all on Jim. Jim, what help do you want with your noble effort to improve?"

"True confession: I'm not good at asking for help. God knows, in this case, I need it." I asked my guys for two things: One, stop me if I start to interrupt someone, and two, fight back when I try to do their jobs for them. They readily agreed.

I woke in the middle of that night soaked in sweat and beset by doubts. *What the hell did I get myself into? What if I fail at this change business? And how am I supposed to know the difference between responsible and too responsible? If I can't make out where the line is, how am I supposed to stay on the right side of it?*

On waking, I was still troubled and preoccupied. I hate to wallow. To beat it out of myself, I jumped on the NordicTrack, the original ski-type machine that I'd held onto all these years. Excruciatingly boring, but it remains a sure-fire way to work up a sweat in twenty minutes. I moved my 8:00 a.m. to make time for that. It helped. With room in my mind for more than just work worries, I thought of Cristine. Maybe she could help.

Trouble at Home

I had always kept work to myself in the belief that I was sparing Cristine. But I decided to bring her into it. Kept pretty much in the dark for twenty-plus years, she nevertheless agreed without giving me any grief. Duly noted, much appreciated. We grabbed breakfast at a fast-food place. In our booth, the noise level wasn't unmanageable. I told her about the two-pronged plan.

"Makes sense to me," she said, "but what's the plan for around here?"

Embarrassed, I confessed, "I hadn't thought of that."

Giving me no credit for honesty, she let me have it. "That's precisely the problem." She was exasperated.

On the defensive, I said, weakly, "So what do you want me to do?"

"Why is it up to me? Look. Let's start with the problem. What do you think it is?" She was demanding but not mean. Even in the heat of the moment, I noticed that.

"Let me think. On weekdays, I'm never around?"

"Yes. Face it: You're an absentee parent."

"That bad? What about the weekends? I'm in play a lot of the time."

"Not really. You're on the phone a lot. You even take calls in the car while the rest of us are sitting there. Put me aside; how do you think the kids feel sitting there made to listen?"

I sighed. *She's right*, I admitted to myself, *but what am I supposed to do about it?* "I've got this big job—"

"You and your big job. Not everyone with a job like yours is out of whack like you. I know that from some of the other wives."

"You're not telling them about us, are you?"

"No, I'm not about to trot out our dirty linen."

Dirty linen: That's what she thinks!

Cristine extracted a commitment from me to get home in time for dinner once a week. That may not sound like much, but on the chosen day, I struggled mightily to defeat the force of habit and extract myself from the office on time. I did not want to disappoint my children, who Cristine had told to expect me home. Nor did I want to risk her wrath.

I kept trying to get home once a week in time for dinner, but my record was spotty. I figured Cristine would cut me some slack. She'd always been understanding. A couple of months went by uneventfully. One weekday night, I went to the kitchen for a glass of water and was about to head back to my office.

Cristine came up to me and announced, "We need to talk." *Uh-oh*, I said to myself.

"Is this the time and the place?" I asked. It was 10:30; I had my head in work.

"There's never a good time." She was right.

I sighed but said, "If you must."

"I must. I'm fed up, Jim." In shock, I reached behind me for a chair. As I sat down without looking, I slid the chair backward and almost landed on my ass.

Those three words, *I'm fed up*, scared me half to death. A mortal fear of being abandoned, deserted, forsaken, lodged itself in the deepest regions of my mind. The alarm bells were so loud I could hardly hear myself think. Finally, I was able to speak. "I had no idea." I barely suppressed the urge to plead, *Don't leave me.*

"I know. That's the problem. Your attention is elsewhere."

"But you and the kids are so important to me. That's why I work so hard, to be responsible to the family."

"You do that very well. Too well. You're gone all week, and what do you do on Saturday morning? Dive into your briefcase. I've been with the kids all week, and at the weekend, I can really use a hand. Do I get it? No, never."

"Why haven't you told me?"

She sat down on the other side of the kitchen table and buried her face in her hands. I went over and put my hand on her shoulder; she shook it off. I stood there, awkward and buffeted by strong feelings I couldn't parcel out. Finally, tear-streaked, she looked up at me.

"Tell me, please," I repeated.

She shook her head. I got her a tissue, which she accepted. She wiped her eyes and blew her nose.

"Jim, you're hopeless. How can someone as smart as you be so stupid?" A note of kindness crept into her voice.

I looked down. It was my turn to get emotional. "Don't shoot me, but I don't understand why it's so hurtful that I work on Saturday mornings."

"What's so hurtful? You act like the kids aren't important, like I'm not important."

So that's it: I've deserted her. I've deserted the children. Here I am, afraid she'll leave me, and all along, I've left her. "I'm such a jerk. Such a jerk. Can you ever forgive me?"

"It's late. That's quite enough for now."

I couldn't sleep, couldn't stop berating myself. *How stupid can you be? Your wife is unhappy. She's unhappy with you. She has been for years, and you had no idea. You couldn't stop being threatened. She put you on notice. You could lose her. Disaster. The whole family would be blown apart.* Just as it was getting light outside, the answer became crystal clear: Don't take her for granted, and don't take the kids for granted. This floated into my brain: *As a father, you're nothing like your father to you.* Cortisol flooded my brain, the body's response to failure. *And for that matter, you're just like your mother—lost to your own children.* Another shot of cortisol.

The very next Saturday morning, it was all I could do to keep from following my natural, habitual tendency to get into my briefcase, but I refrained. I could tell Cristine was pleased. But on the fourth or fifth Saturday morning, I fell back into my natural order—without realizing it, if you can believe that. In the days that followed, I got the impression that Cristine was unhappy, but I didn't put two and two together. When she had a free moment, I asked, "Are you okay?" I was genuinely concerned.

"I'm fine," she said, firmly but, I thought, disingenuously.

"You don't seem that way." I was concerned about her. "What is it? Is it me?"

"Never mind," she said evasively.

Now I was sure something was wrong, but I wasn't able to pry it out of her. Later in the day, I approached her again. This time, the floodgates opened. "Am I chopped liver? Are the kids chopped liver?" she said bitterly.

I slapped my hand against my forehead. "How stupid of me." I couldn't tell what I felt worse about, relapsing or hurting her so badly. *You fool,* I said to myself. *You clueless bastard.* I took her hands, and she let me, reluctantly. She must have seen the pained expression on my face. The kids had finished watching their program and had started to run around. So we decided to continue the conversation over breakfast at a nearby fast-food place that Saturday.

After we'd finished our bacon-and-egg biscuits, I said, "I've given it a lot of thought. The reality is I am as dumb as a farm animal. Would you please put a ring in my nose and lead me around the farmyard like a mule?" Rarely did I ask for help, but this time, threat and desperation drove me to it.

"What does that mean?" Cristine asked. "If, come Saturday morning, you don't report promptly for duty, I grab hold of that ring and lead you none too gently to the correct field?"

"That's exactly what it means," I said.

She laughed, the best music there is. So that became the new order of things. It wasn't just that I had to take my place in it. I wanted to.

"How's the plan going?" At first, I didn't know what she meant. Then I clicked in—my work goals.

I filled her in, and finished by saying, "I'm seeing that I've got an overblown sense of responsibility."

"Unevenly applied." I wanted to ask what she meant but thought, *Better figure this out yourself, Bub.* But I couldn't. I looked at her helplessly.

"Overactive at work. At home . . ."

I got my back up. "Are you saying I'm not a good provider?"

"Of course not. You're a great provider."

"Because it's not just putting a roof over our heads and food on the table. It's building up savings, so the sky can never fall in on us, like it pretty much did after my dad died."

"Yes, I know," she said. "But aren't we already there?"

"Maybe. It's hard for me to judge. It's like there's never enough."

"I didn't know that. Look, I know you care about me and that you care about the kids. But—" Her shoulders sagged. "I don't want to rub your nose in it." She looked at me, wanting, I thought, a hand.

"I'll spare you: It's me not showing up."

"Thank you, yes. What's so compelling about work? I know it's stimulating, and you'd like to advance—"

"Putting aside financial security, it's achievement." I thought to tell her about my successful quest to bowl 300. I had never told her about it. She was impressed that I was able to do it; she was very good that way. "It's being able to count. That way, you can tell whether what you've done is worth anything."

It was hard to put my finger on it, and I expected her to appreciate that. But, no, I got a completely different response.

"Pity me," she said poignantly and a bit bitterly. "How am I supposed to have a sense of worth carpooling, preparing meals, keeping the house in order—repetitive, thankless tasks? I don't regret staying home with the kids, but some days, I long for my finance job. Anyway, now I get it."

"I don't envy you. Shouldn't we be getting back? The babysitter is expecting us." I slid along the seat and started to get up.

"Not so fast," she said.

I sat back down with a thud. "What is it? Didn't we do good work?"

"We're not out of the woods yet," she said. "As far as I'm concerned, we've just taken the first few steps."

"Oh, I'd been keyed on those steps. What do you have in mind?" I thought, *Oh no, not marriage counseling.*

"Marriage counseling."

My face fell, I'm sure. *Gretchen is one thing*, I said to myself. *That's one on one. I can handle that. But there's no telling when some counselor—a complete stranger, I don't care how highly she's recommended—starts mucking around with the two of us. She, or he, could dredge up crap that's better left at the bottom.*

"Haven't we done pretty well by ourselves?" I said. "Today, for example, and that time in the kitchen. What do you think?"

She kept me in suspense for what seemed like an eternity. "Yes, so far we've done pretty well."

I breathed a private sigh of relief. "So, can we give it a try, by ourselves? If it doesn't work, well, then we can get professional help."

"Okay, we'll give it a try."

We arranged to talk away from the kids at a set time every weekend. From the way she handled the crisis in our marriage to the way she dealt with me and my failings and failures, my eyes were opened even more to how capable she was, just not in areas where I was strong. I came away feeling deeply that she and the kids really did mean the world to me. *Why then*, I thought, *do you devote so little time to them? You know why: You're obsessed with work.*

Change Effort at Work

At work, I made headway on my second goal, to hear people out, even when it meant digging my fingernails into the palm of my hand while they spoke. To dispel the urge altogether, that little wave of my head worked sometimes. Tracking helped too: I kept a running tally of the number of times I interrupted. I arranged with Vince to signal me when I interrupted and, if I didn't pick up the sign, to break in. It was a constant struggle.

But my number one goal, to let other people lead, not to do

other people's work for them, I often lost. This is what I was afraid of, that I'd fail at improving. The team kept up their end of the bargain. They pushed back when I took over. But that too often proved fruitless, pointless. One by one, they gave up. I didn't blame them. At home, I had been able to make adjustments, but there, I had a full-time enforcer. At work, Vince notwithstanding, there was no such thing—nothing with sharp teeth in it.

Gretchen heard about my difficulty letting go. We arranged to talk. "For one thing, it's just quicker to do it myself," I explained.

"That's ironic: Your brainpower works against you. Do you fight the impulse to step in?"

"Of course. You don't think I'm taking it lying down?" I said good-naturedly.

"Of course not. Sorry to imply otherwise. Maybe it's something deeper? Do you want to go there?"

A great one for bearing my burdens in silence, I made an exception with her. She had a counseling degree. She was well equipped. Beyond that, I didn't know much about her and her life. Then again, I'd never thought to ask.

"I've had glimmers," I said. "Here's one. I'm realizing that I equate turning over responsibility with asking for help. But I'm not somebody who asks for help. Ever."

"Which leaves you where?"

"Right back at the thing I'm trying to fix. Putting too much on myself. Like you said, that's why my shoulders are stooped. I'll keep at it."

I tried, to no avail. So a month later, I called on Gretchen once again. I surprised myself by asking for so much of her help when that had not been my way. "Responsibility clings to me like flypaper," I said.

"What do you mean?"

"Do I need to spell it out for you?" Beats me why I was cranky. To her credit, she didn't respond. I sighed. "Sorry about that. Responsibility lands on me unbidden, and I can't get rid of it. How's that?"

"It helps. Any idea how that came to be?"

"Like I told you, my dad died when I was growing up. You know how that story goes."

"Yeah, sure, but what matters is how it affected you in your life. Can you get some time to yourself in the next few days? To reflect."

"Sure, this weekend. Cristine will understand." But a little voice in my head said, *Don't be so sure. It'll probably test her patience.*

"Good. Go off by yourself, away from the house. In nature is ideal. A coffee shop will do. And go back over that time. Recall it in as much detail as you can. Take a pad, write it down."

"Never done that before. Avoided the whole thing."

"Exactly. That's my point." I got Cristine's permission to skip church on Sunday to do my soul-searching. She was generous about it.

Flashback in The Bleachers

I went to the park, sat in the bleachers of the baseball field, and reminisced. My father, who'd played high school baseball—which

I'd planned to do too—would take me to a nearby field and put me through my paces—fastballs, change-ups, curves, bunting. He didn't say much, just a word here and there. "Bat back." "Wait for a good pitch." "Opposite field." He brought a wire basket full of hardballs. When it was empty, I'd run around the outfield picking them up. He did the infield.

On the way home, we'd stop at a McDonald's for something to drink. "Slugger"—that's what my dad called me during baseball season—"this coming season, pitchers will be throwing a lot harder, and you're young for this age bracket. It'll be an adjustment. So I'll start throwing faster."

"Did you do any of that today? I had trouble getting the bat around on some pitches."

"Yeah, I did; yeah, you did. With practice, it'll come to you." That was the great thing about my dad. He'd put in the time and kept the advice to a minimum.

When my father died, it blew a hole in my sense of well-being. The youthful energy I'd always taken for granted drained out of me. I slept practically the whole next day and then lay around in bed. I was in my pajamas the whole time. No appetite—that was a switch. A couple of my friends came by, but I sent them away. I had someone cover my route.

When it came time for relatives, all from out of town, to arrive for the funeral, I had to get dressed. My mother and sister yanked at my arms and legs to haul me out of bed. They left the room for me to change clothes. They returned to find me sitting on the edge of the bed in my underwear. "C'mon, Jimmy," my sister said, appealing to me.

"Hop to it," my mother had ordered.

"Okay, okay," I'd said, somehow ready to cooperate. *Hop to it* was my father's line.

The Monday after the funeral, I went back to school and started delivering papers again. I had stopped moping around as if a switch had been flipped. I heard our next-door neighbor, a friend of the family, remark approvingly to my mother, "What a trouper!" That same neighbor asked me more than once, "How are you doing, Jimmy?," a note of concern in her voice. My heavy sadness must have been palpable.

The funeral behind us, a new social order had set in, radically different, most unwelcome. Family dinners—shot to hell. Everyone fended or foraged for themselves. My mother was around even less. Oh, she was home alright but either in Mom's world or in an alcohol-induced haze. My sister was off with friends or in her room. We had never been close—somehow the three-year difference in age put us on separate tracks—and hard times didn't draw us together. Isolated in my own home, I'd stand in the kitchen and suffer terrible pangs of loneliness that I told nobody about.

After a couple of weeks, my mother came to me, saying that the car, a 1975 Volvo station wagon, was squealing. She asked me to take a look. My father had done all the work on the car—and the house. After dinner, he'd go out to the garage, and I'd tag along. He let me change the oil and help with repairs.

But I didn't hop to it, and a few days later, the car overheated. Luckily, it had happened just a few blocks from home. I walked over, nervous about handling it by myself and unsure that I could. I lifted the hood and tugged at the fan belt. Just as I'd suspected, it was loose. I was relieved it wasn't a failed water pump. The toolbox was in its usual spot in the trunk. I tightened the fan belt. Then I unscrewed the cap on the radiator and refilled it. My dad always kept a gallon container of water back there. I felt good to be equal to the task but sick at having to do what my dad would have done, to replace him. What choice did I have?

My mother continued to drink to excess. When that happened, it usually fell to me to look after her. My sister, sad to say, was too busy feeling sorry for herself.

Despite my mother's alcohol problem, she had managed to hold onto her job as a supervisor at the local grocery store. Thank goodness for that: I don't know what we'd have done without her paycheck. She quit drinking a few years later, after I left for college.

Maybe a month after my dad died, she returned home from work and called out to me. I'd been sitting on the back porch, whittling a branch down to nothing. I came into the kitchen, and she said, "Sit down. I've got good news for you."

I sat down, wondering what this good news could be. Cautiously, I got my hopes up. "What, Mom?"

"I got you a job at the grocery store. The owner is taking pity on us; he's willing to pay you off the books, since you're not sixteen. We need the extra money."

"What are the hours?"

"After school 'til six and Saturdays. He'll pay you just below minimum wage."

I had jerked up from the chair. "Good news?! Don't you realize what this means?! I can't play baseball. Dad would never do this to me. He knew how important baseball is to me." I had always dreamed of playing on the high school varsity. Coach B thought I had a good chance. So did my father, who ought to know. My dream was shot to hell. The camaraderie, teammates ribbing each other, gutting it out—all that was swept away by the vicious broom of necessity. I ran out the screen door, letting it slam behind me.

I'd hated the grocery store job with a vengeance. Restocking shelves, I slashed open cardboard boxes with the box cutter. *Take that!* I said to myself. *Take that!* But as time went on, the heat seeped out. *It is what it is*, I took to saying to myself. I must have sensed that fighting it—the job, what I had to do for my mother, losing baseball and hanging out with friends—got me nowhere. All that bad feeling must have gotten buried like nuclear waste stored in deep rock formations, durable repositories. It became like something that happened before I was born, something I'd heard about but hadn't actually experienced. That sounds ridiculous, but my mind had arranged to treat my losses like ancient history—up until this moment, overlooking the empty baseball field, until talking about my way of leading and revisiting the past came together like two long-lost cousins that happened to sit next to each other on a plane flight.

I had moved on, and I was grateful for that, proud of myself for not dwelling on the past. But I had given myself no credit for that. It just happened that way, like a kid arm wrestling with his father: Instantly, his arm gets thrown down on the table.

Couldn't Wait to Tell Gretchen

I made time on my calendar to meet with Gretchen the very next day.

"So?" she said in a voice both tender and interested.

"Too painful for words." Literally. I wasn't sure I could speak to it, despite Gretchen's inviting manner. I stopped; it was awkward. She waited patiently. I hit on something I could tell her. "When Cristine heard what I planned to do, not work but reflect, she gave me a special dispensation. I could spend the whole day, in place of going to church with her and the kids. Sitting in the bleachers, I took out my pad, and it all came rushing back." I bent over in pain.

She walked over and placed her hand on my back. It was a bit strange yet comforting. I sat back up, and she returned to her chair. I looked over at her. She was attentive, but more than that, I could tell she cared; she cared about me. So I let her in on what had happened. Tears came to her eyes. My eyes followed suit.

"But Gretchen," I said after a moment, "where does all that leave me?" I could tell she wanted me to say more. "I'm still stuck. I still don't know what keeps me from offloading responsibility."

"Fear," she said, "is the enemy of thought and action."

That took me aback. I didn't think of myself as having fears. I had been toughened by life, calloused. But her statement got me thinking. "Well, now that you mention it, I live in fear of getting fired. Always have. I try to tell myself it won't happen, but I can't talk myself out of it."

"That's the way with fear. It's a poor listener. But let's say you were fired. Are you financially secure, may I ask?"

"I've made sure of that. When we had trouble making ends meet, I vowed never to be in dire financial constraints again. All along, I've put money away."

"Good, so money isn't a concern. Still, you clutch responsibility like it's a life preserver."

"Yeah, I do."

"You once spoke of Atlas. Have you read *Atlas Shrugged*?"

"Yeah, it's one of my favorite books. Do you know the punch line?" She gestured for me to tell her. "Well, all the productive people walk off the job, and the world falls apart."

She looked at me, expectantly. I didn't know what she wanted me to say. When I stayed silent, at a loss, she spelled it out for me. "You've as much as said you live in fear your world will fall apart."

That struck me like a blow to the head. I felt blood rush into my face. I wasn't just shocked; I was embarrassed to be so slow on the uptake.

Seeing my distress, Gretchen got up from her chair. I rose to meet her, and she embraced me as if were a child. I'm not the sort to hug, certainly not at work, but I gave myself up to it. As I relaxed into it, I thought of Cristine and how much it means to me to be loved by her. Maybe that's why I proved able to keep my head out of my briefcase on Saturday morning and get home in time for dinner on a weekday.

Standing apart from each other, Gretchen asked, "Do you feel for the guy living in mortal fear?"

I wasn't prepared for that either. "Fear! No. Are you calling me weak?"

"You certainly were strong at that time and very functional. But it wasn't the whole story, was it?"

"I guess not." I looked up at the ceiling, deep in thought. "I suppose I do feel for the guy. He's been afraid, but he couldn't afford to know that. So that's why I couldn't let go. Fear wouldn't let me, fear that if I didn't do everything, my world would fall apart."

"So now you know what you're up against?" she said.

"I do. And I'll be on the alert for it; you can be sure of that." I thanked her heartily and shut the door to my office.

Leaning way back in my desk chair, I thought, *Ah, the wrestling match: Now when my right arm reaches for a piece of work that isn't mine to do, my left hand can do something about it. Now it's a fair fight. What was that my father said when I struggled to adjust to fast pitching? "With practice, it will come to you."*

Super! If I can cut out this Atlas business at work, I can be the husband and the father I want to be. There's nothing like Cristine's laugh when she's pleased with me.

LESSONS FOR LEADERS

As people, we change because we're forced to. Perhaps adversity or outright tragedy strikes, either us or a loved one, and we change our ways or our way of looking at life. In addition, we can bring change on ourselves because we want to. But that doesn't mean you will have an easy time of it.

Willpower Can Work

Your boss says, "You're always late to my staff meeting. Get there on time." And you do. You're newly married, and your spouse says, "Will you please put the cap back on the toothpaste?" And you do. You decide to go last in your staff meeting, to get the benefit of everyone's thinking. And you do. Having fallen into the habit of having two glasses of wine with dinner, you decide one is enough. And you do. Think it, and it's done. Because you have enough self-command and self-mastery.

But Often Willpower Isn't Enough

Then we're like a ship run aground on an unseen shoal. You make a good-faith effort to improve, but a hidden force restrains you, won't release its grip on you. Or you make headway, only to fall back, relapse. What do you have to show for your efforts? Nothing. It's frustrating, discouraging—embarrassing even.

Find Out What You're Up Against

Do you know what the problem is, why you hit a snag? You need to find out what you're up against. Often it's mindset. On your mental map, is "drive for results" as big as Brazil while "patience with people when they occasionally screw up" is no bigger than Lichtenstein? The way you assign or allocate importance is fateful. What you assign low importance you won't do much of. What you assign high importance you do a lot of, and you're probably overdoing it; you think the more, the better.

Strong forces have their way too—overheated ambition, undue fear, unrealistic expectations, unchecked ego needs, disabling self-doubt. Worst case: The door to what you're up against is closed. The fear of knowing defeats your need to know.

The Fight Is with Yourself

Speaking of mindset, our mind is often set in its ways. People believe what they believe, the ancient Greek philosopher, Heraclitus, said. They have ears, but they cannot hear; they have eyes, but they cannot see.

To improve is to grapple with yourself, but it's often not a fair fight. Your interest in improving is overmatched by the mental factors and forces that made you what you are and that keep you that way. Have you heard this one? If one person says you're stubborn as a mule, ignore him. But if three people do, go out and buy a harness and a bale of hay.

You say you want to raise your game? Fine, we'll take a look at your play on the field and have you make some adjustments. But, equally, we check out your mental game if you are to have a fighting chance of playing better.

Factor In Childhood Influences

As the adage goes, the way the twig is bent, so grows the tree. Put another way, the child is parent to the adult. Growing up, what were the *dos* and *don'ts*? Who were your role models, good and bad? What came naturally, and what did not? Also, the ratio of favorable to unfavorable growing-up conditions is always indicative. A high ratio: You probably have a solid interior foundation, but if it's low, you may, to one degree or another, have difficulty functioning.

Some of your tendencies are no doubt innate. Short of a DNA sample, you can ask people who knew you when you were a very young child and the world had yet to get its mitts on you. Were you mild-mannered and accommodating or strong-minded and aggressive? Were you a born go-getter, or did you cling to your mother's skirts?

Be Open To A Character Shift

No, a leopard can't change its spots. But, by evolving, the dark spots can come to be lighter, and the tawny background color can be brought out more. The leopard is still unmistakably a leopard but is recognizably different, a leopard of a different character.

A character shift is a change in emphasis, a major one. Let's say that, to date, you've placed way too much emphasis on one way of leading and way too little on its counterpart. Perhaps you relied heavily on your own intellect and energy and have yet to learn there is power in empowering. Not just letting people do their jobs—under your direction, of course—but letting them influence you—selectively, of course. It's a struggle to make that shift, but you stick with it and power through.

Grappling, you may have an epiphany, a lightning-strike self-realization. Or you may experience a catharsis. But just as thunderstorms don't come out of nowhere, there is a gradual build-up to self-realization or emotional release. Leader and guide together wade through the yawning complexity of your leadership style, your life experience, and the way your mind works and emerge with a potent unifying idea. Oliver Wendell Holmes once said, "I wouldn't give a fig for the simplicity on this side of complexity, but I would give my life for the simplicity on the other side of complexity." It's a clarity that sparks natural energy for change. You see the light, and you feel the heat that compels change.

Grappling with yourself can be hard work, but it can be "pleasant in its unpleasantness," as one leader put it to me. It's analogous to doing intervals, running or swimming or biking. During the high-intensity bursts when for ten or twenty or thirty seconds, you're going all-out—past the point where you want to stop. It's borderline obnoxious but, in its own way, satisfying. And it makes for a better you: Your mitochondria are healthier, and mitochondria deliver power to the cell.

Heed The Positive Feedback

Positive feedback leverages in the worthy struggle to improve. That's not what most leaders think, though. They think the active ingredient is negative feedback. "This is what I can do something about," they typically say. They're not wrong. But what they don't realize is that positive feedback is just as potent, just as useful, and just as capable of producing growth. And it's even better at serving another purpose, arguably a higher purpose: boosting your confidence. Isn't self-confidence the big prize? If you—like so many of us—underestimate how good you are, how accomplished, either across the board or on a dimension that matters greatly to you, an uptick in your self-regard will do wonders for you. As payback for holding yourself in higher regard, you naturally alleviate, ameliorate, or outright fix some of the negatives, which spring in the first place from a lack of confidence.

But there's a fly in the ointment. Practically all of us are thirsty for validation, but we're reluctant to drink from that cup. The culprit? Often, it's humility, drilled into our brains as children: "Don't get a swelled head" or "You're too big for your britches." Are you one of those people who won't let the positives sink in without a struggle strung out over time?

Buttress Yourself—With Structure

Like any project, your change effort needs structure. What are the goals (not too many), actions, and tracking mechanisms? This is a regimen so familiar to leaders that it doesn't need to be laid out in detail here. I might add that not everyone needs an implementation apparatus. All they need is to see it, and they retain it and make it happen.

Structure takes other forms. Let's say that, in one-on-one meetings with direct reports, you're not tough enough on performance. You make up for that deficit by instituting quarterly reviews with the team. One by one, each person's results against objectives for the quarter are posted. Gaps speak for themselves. Little needs to be said except "Get after it."

Buttress Yourself—With Staffing

Staffing is another form of empowering. You may well need someone on your staff who has what you lack, a counterbalance, as you're trying to improve at something, in the meantime, or a counterweight, someone who either keeps you from overstepping or makes you do what you otherwise wouldn't.

Involve Your Partner

Your partner, your spouse, who knows you better than any professional, can be a big boost to your efforts to change. But the relationship has to be strong enough. I find that when couples, especially those with kids at home, lack chemistry, it's not necessarily because the couple is incompatible. Often, it's because they don't take time for themselves—quality time. The problem is structural, not interpersonal. The remedy is regular time together away from the house, both to stay connected and as co-CEOs of the family, to talk over the issues of the day.

The other thing is the partner must have a voice. Often, they do not. Some leaders, in the name of work–life balance, don't talk about work at home. That wall has to come down. There's a bigger obstacle, though: The partner—and, in particular, the stay-at-home person, man or woman—ends up in a one-down position. That power imbalance needs to be rectified and can be rectified if a guide presides.

Make A Parallel Change Outside Of Work

The roles of supervisor and parent often run parallel. If you attempt to be less dictatorial at work, you could make the same attempt with your kids. The efforts in two different spheres reinforce each other.

You May Need A Guide

Working on yourself usually means mindset work, which is hard to do well on your own and can quickly get uncomfortable. This is where a guide comes in, someone who knows the terrain of self-work for leaders, who brings out the leader to good effect, who doesn't push too hard when there is resistance and instead backs up and comes at it from a different angle, who is skilled at landing the individual in a better place, and who ensures safe passage.

About the guides in these several narratives, a prepublication reviewer noted the frequent use of "guiding questions." It so happened that right after the book was completed, I heard basically the same thing about myself from several people at work and outside of work. A friend, for example, cited "the ability to draw others out by posing questions and genuinely attending to the answers, making for a special quality of conversation." A colleague observed that I "listen perceptively and question directly—to get to the gist of the conversation." I was surprised by how many people brought up my question-driven way of engaging. But, in one way, I can relate. Moment to moment in meetings or conversations, I'm thinking, *Do I ask, or do I tell?* It's tempting to show off what you know or be the one with the answer. Isn't it better when people can tumble to it themselves?

ACKNOWLEDGMENTS

E very one of the narratives in this book I sent to several people for review. But first a given narrative had to make it past my wife, Rebecca, a discerning and candid reader.

Several readers have been with me the whole way: Lynda Bryson, my long-time and multitalented assistant; David DeVries; Sarah Schaible; Michael Walters; and Jay Talbot, who reviewed all of the stories. Many other people critiqued one or another piece:

Brad Smith, Karen Talmadge, Jim Hoffman, Lawrence Stibbards, Ron Ashkenas, Rob Kaiser, John Figueroa, Samir Malik, Danish Munir, Lisa Franchi, Sanjeev Verma, Randy Battat, Sandy LaGrega, Angelo LaGrega, Ricardo Berckemeyer, Gabriel Sander—as well as my first wife, Merrily Kaplan, who had a big influence on certain pieces and on my confidence that I could write novelistically. Special thanks to my children, Josh, Emily, and Andrew, for their support.

Starting out, I had not the faintest idea of what it meant to write fiction. "Show people in action," Chris Bergonzi told me. Chris is the long-time editor of my professional writing. Next, Benee Knauer took me in hand, schooling me especially in structure and character development, as we worked our way through all eight narratives—a combo of editing and tutoring. Then, by chance, I met Walter Bode, formerly the editor-in-chief of Grove Press and an editor at Viking Press. He and I iterated on every story from every angle and at every level, raising my game as we went along. Then, when I thought I was done working on the narratives, Henry Devries came along and added choice finishing touches.

I also want to thank my many excellent Kaplan DeVries colleagues, who encouraged me in this writing project and alongside whom I have refined my craft as helper.

ABOUT THE AUTHOR

BOB KAPLAN is the founder of Kaplan DeVries, advisors to senior people on leadership. He has a bachelor's degree in English and a doctorate in organizational behavior from Yale, and lives in New York City with his wife, Becky.

That's Bob on the back cover. He had no idea the photograph was being taken. ⓒ Karel Steiner

For all inquiries, please contact Bob at
bobkaplan@kaplandevries.com.